MW01120503

Criminal Justice
Recent Scholarship

Edited by
Nicholas P. Lovrich

A Series from LFB Scholarly

Intimate Partner Violence among Adolescents
Causes and Correlates

Valerie A. Clark

LFB Scholarly Publishing LLC
El Paso 2013

X

Library of Congress Cataloging-in-Publication Data

Clark, Valerie A., 1981-
   Intimate partner violence among adolescents : causes and correlates /
Valerie A. Clark.
      p. cm.
   Includes bibliographical references and index.
   ISBN 978-1-59332-589-3 (hardcover : alk. paper)
   1. Intimate partner violence--United States. 2. Dating violence--
United
States. 3. Abused teenagers--United States. 4. Teenage girls--Abuse
of--United States. 5. Abusive men--United States. I. Title.
   HV6626.2.C55 2013
   362.88--dc23

                                  2012040466

ISBN 978-1-59332-589-3

Printed on acid-free 250-year-life paper.

Manufactured in the United States of America.

Table of Contents

v

CHAPTER 1

General Violence and Intimate Partner Violence among Adolescents: Similarities and Differences

INTRODUCTION

Adolescence is a time for romance, and sometimes violence. By age 17, about 70% of adolescents have been involved in a romantic relationship within the prior 18 months (Collins 2003). Although these relationships were once thought of as fleeting and shallow, research suggests that often they can be long-lasting and meaningful (Carver, Joyner, and Udry 2003). Most adolescents involved in romantic relationships have publicly acknowledged their relationships to friends and they have met the parents of their partners, both of which actions are considered major milestones in relationships. However, for some adolescents romantic involvement can be harmful. According to the Centers for Disease Control, adolescent intimate partner violence in the U.S. is at an all-time high with nearly one-in-11 adolescents reporting abuse within the prior 12 months (National Center for Injury Prevention 2006). Nearly 30% of teens report psychological abuse (Halpern et al. 2001; Mulford and Giordano 2008).

The purpose of this research is to examine the relationship between adolescent intimate partner violence (IPV[1]), violent offending, and violent victimization over time and to address critical limitations in the literature. The relatively large body of research on the correlates and consequences of adolescent IPV suffers from three major deficiencies—namely, a lack of longitudinal analyses, samples that are generally limited to female victims, and the failure to consider the influence of friendship networks.

The research reported here addresses these limitations and provides a more complete examination of adolescent IPV. Specifically, this study addresses five research questions: (1) Are early violent offending and violent victimization risk factors for IPV? (2) Does the relationship between IPV and other deviant behaviors persist after controlling for early behaviors?; (3) Do peer network characteristics influence these relationships?; (4) Do these relationships vary for male and female adolescents?; and (5) Does the relationship between IPV victimization, general violence, and other deviant behaviors vary depending on whether the relationship abuse was mutual (i.e., both partners reported IPV victimization) or one-sided (i.e., only one partner reported IPV victimization).

Besides these basic objectives, the present research has a larger of goal of addressing the extent to which IPV is similar to and different from other forms of violent victimization. Some violence scholars (e.g., Felson 2002, 2006) have argued that IPV should not be examined separately from other forms of violence. Conversely, many feminist scholars (e.g., Dobash and Dobash 1979) contend that IPV is a separate form of violence that has unique origins, victims, and consequences. This research examines whether IPV follows a pattern unique to that of general violence, whether the patterns are the same, or whether general violence and IPV are both similar and different under certain circumstances.

By answering these questions this study furthers our understanding of teen dating violence, which has become an important topic of study among criminologists (Mulford and Giordano 2008), mainstream

---

[1] Note: In this monograph, the phrase "intimate partner violence" (IPV) refers to any instance of partner-directed aggression, both physical and non-physical.

observers in the media (Olson 2009), and multiple governmental agencies, including the CDC. Also, this study is the first research project examining teen dating violence to approximate Johnson's (2008) domestic violence typology, which distinguishes between four separate types of IPV. To meet these objectives, this research uses the first three waves of the National Longitudinal Study of Adolescent Health (Add Health), including the secure romantic partnership data. The longitudinal design of Add Health allows for an examination of the effects of intimate partner violence over an extended period. In addition to detailed information on romantic relationships, the Add Health data also include information on the households in which the adolescents live, the schools they attend, the friendship networks to which they belong, and the communities in which they reside. These data allow for a thorough examination of adolescent romantic partnerships.

LITERATURE REVIEW

This project expands upon existing research on the relationship between adolescent IPV and deviant behavior by integrating the following lines of research: (1) the prevalence and consequences of adult IPV; (2) the correlates and consequences of adolescent IPV; (3) the "gendered" and "violence" perspectives of IPV; (4) the influence of peer networks on offending and victimization; and, (5) the role of gender in offending and victimization. The first part of this literature review describes the research on IPV among adults, followed by a review of research on abuse among adolescents, and highlights the limitations of this research. Lastly, the importance of examining peer influence and gender in these analyses is outlined.

Adult Intimate Partner Violence
Only in the past 30 to 40 years has domestic violence between adults been recognized as a serious problem (Dobash and Dobash 1992; Federal Bureau of Investigation 2005; Stark 2007). The women's movement of the late 1960s and 1970s in Britain and the U.S. addressed issues relating to equal rights for women and provided the "base of membership and the overall perspective" for many social movements, including the battered women's movement (Dobash and Dobash 1992, 16). The recognition of spousal abuse as a serious

problem, rather than a male privilege, came from other movements that recognized oppressed groups, the transition towards women's paid labor, and the public's long-standing aversion to violence (FBI 2005; Straus and Gelles 1990). Beginning with the debut of two women's shelters in Minnesota and Massachusetts in the early 1970s, the U.S. battered women's movement had the three main goals of providing assistance to victims, of challenging male violence against women, and of improving the position of women in society.

Today the battered women's movement consists of women's shelters all around the world, intervention efforts for women stuck in abusive relationships, counseling for survivors, a shift in how violence against women is portrayed in the media and defined in the law, and an abundance of research that describes both the problem and how to address it (Stark 2007, 6). In the U.S. currently shelters and other outreach programs for victims of domestic violence serve more than three million women and children annually. The battered women's movement has emerged in the U.S. legal system through a hardened stance towards individuals accused of abusing their partners, the recognition of marital rape under the law, several reforms in how police officers respond to domestic violence situations, access to protection from abuse orders from the courts, and specialized courts meant to deal specifically with family conflict (Dobash and Dobash 1992; Stark 2007).

Despite the prevention and intervention efforts of the battered women's movement, domestic violence continues to be a serious problem and rates of violence have remained nearly constant over the past 30 years. A special report by the Federal Bureau of Investigation (FBI), which examined National Incident Based Reporting System (NIBRS) data, found that 1.5 million out of the 3.5 million violent interpersonal confrontations that included identifiable victims involved familial relationships (FBI 2005). More than 60% of these family-related incidents were committed by intimate partners. According to the National Violence Against Women (NVAW) Survey, a nationally representative telephone survey of 8,000 men and 8,000 women conducted between 1995 and 1996, about 25% of surveyed women and 8% of surveyed men were raped and/or assaulted by an intimate partner (Tjaden and Thoennes 2000). Results from the 1998 National Crime

Victimization Survey (NCVS) echoed this finding. Estimates derived from these data sources revealed that one million violent crimes were committed against individuals by current and former significant others, and most of the victims of these crimes were women (Rennison and Welchans 2000). Johnson (1995, 2008) estimated that two to six million women in the U.S. experience violence by a male partner each year.

Several other studies have indicated that women are more commonly the victims of intimate partner violence than men (e.g., Dobash et al. 1992; Dobash and Dobash 1992; FBI 2005; Kimmel 2002; Stark 2007). For example, based on a study of emergency room visits in 1994, the Bureau of Justice Statistics found that nearly 40% of emergency room visitors being treated for violent victimization were women, and 36% of these women were victimized by an intimate partner (Rand 1997). According to the NVAW survey, "women were 22.5 times more likely [than men] to report being raped, 2.9 times more likely to report being physically assaulted, and 8.2 times more likely to report being stalked" by an intimate partner at some point in their lives (Tjaden and Thoennes 2000, 151).

Women are also more likely to be killed by their intimate partners compared to men. Between 1976 and 2005, the offender and victim were current or former intimate partners in about 11% of all homicides (Fox and Zawitz 2010). About 33% of female homicide victims were murdered by current or former intimate partners, compared to only 3% of male homicide victims. Although homicides committed by intimate partners have been declining over the past 30 years, females still account for a large majority (75%) of intimate partner homicide victims (Rennison 2003). Besides non-fatal and fatal injuries, other consequences of IPV for female victims include chronic pain, gynecological disorders, and poor mental health (e.g., depression, suicidal thoughts, post-traumatic stress disorder; Goodwin, Chandler, and Meisel 2003; Meisel, Chandler, and Menees 2003; see Campbell 2002 for a review).

Gender Asymmetry in Couple Violence

All of the studies above have found that women are the primary victims of domestic violence. However, one of the longest-running debates among feminist and violence scholars concerns the question of gender symmetry in couple violence: Are men and women equally abusive towards one another in intimate relationships? Opponents of gender symmetry have argued that men monopolize all forms of violence, especially domestic violence (Dobash et al. 1992). Why, they ask, are women disproportionately represented in shelters, calls to police for protection from abuse, and in emergency rooms as a result of male violence (Kimmel 2002)? Further, how is it that men are far more likely to use violence in every other arena of life and not in the household?

Dobash and colleagues (1992) have argued that claims of gender symmetry in spousal abuse are over-stated, and that the motives behind male and female partner abuse tend to differ significantly. Men generally perpetrate partner abuse in order to control and sometimes terrorize their partners, while women engage in violence in self-defense. Indeed, several studies relying upon data from court records, calls to the police, emergency room visits, and women's shelters have found that women are much more likely to be the victims of spousal abuse than men (e.g., Byles 1978; Dobash and Dobash 1979, 1992; Levinger 1966; O'Brien 1971; Rand 1997; Stark 2007).

The abuse described in the preceding paragraphs is consistent with what Stark (2007) calls "coercive control." Coercive control consists of repeated demonstrations of dominance and control by men over women that are sometimes coupled with minor and serious acts of violence. Demonstrations of power and control may include isolation from others, economic deprivation, limits on everyday needs such as food and water, and humiliation. Coercive control typically involves "microregulation" and "microsurveillance" coupled with physical violence over long periods of time, and it relies on the vulnerability and inequality of women. Stark argues that rates of partner abuse towards women have remained stable over the past 30 years. He maintains that the reason official statistics show a decline in rates of IPV is that police, the courts, and the public look only at serious instances of violence and fail to take the whole pattern of abuse into account.

Gender Symmetry in Couple Violence

Proponents of gender symmetry in couple violence argue that men and women resort to violence in relationships at similar rates, and maintain that couple violence is often mutual (Straus 1999; Straus and Gelles

1990). The roots of this argument are found in the 1975 National Family Violence Survey (NFVS), a study in which 2,143 married or cohabitating persons were interviewed about family conflicts that occurred within the preceding year (Straus 1977, 1980). Only one partner and one randomly selected child from the household were interviewed about events that occurred during the year leading up to the interview. To assess family violence, the NFVS employed the Conflict Tactics Scales (CTS). Respondents were asked how they responded to family conflicts within the previous year, and they could choose from a list of 18 acts that ranged from non-violent behavior ("discussed an issue calmly") to violent behavior ("beat him/her/you up"). The respondents were asked how frequently they committed each act during an argument, and how often they received this treatment from their partner within the previous year.

Based on the survey results, Straus concluded that not only do husbands and wives engage in violence at similar rates, the wives perpetrate violence at a higher rate than their husbands. These results were replicated in a 1985 version of the same study (Straus 1990), and several other studies that used the CTS have found that women perpetrate relationship violence at rates similar to males (e.g., McNeely and Mann 1990; Schafer, Caetano, and Clark 1998; Steinmetz 1987; Steinmetz and Lucca 1988).

Opponents and proponents of gender symmetry are able to provide empirical evidence to support their respective positions because each side of the debate has relied on different sources of data to measure different phenomena (Dobash et al. 1992; Johnson 1995; Johnson and Ferraro 2000; Kimmel 2002; Straus 1999). Proponents of gender symmetry obtain their data from "family conflict surveys" (Straus 1999). These surveys consist of nationally representative household surveys, including the NFVS described above (e.g., Straus 1977, 1980; Straus and Gelles 1990) and the National Survey of Families and Households (Sweet, Bumpass, and Call 1988), as well as smaller surveys of college students, dating couples, convenience samples solicited from local advertisements, and clinical studies of couples in therapy (for a full review, see Archer 2000; Fiebert 1997). Most of these surveys question one partner about incidents of violence in the previous year, including less serious forms of violence that are unlikely to come to the attention of police. Surveys that employ the CTS provide overwhelming support for gender symmetry in couple violence (Fiebert 1997; Kimmel 2002).

Opponents of the gender symmetry perspective have argued that family conflict surveys, and more specifically the CTS, are deeply flawed for at least five specific reasons. First, the CTS does not contain questions about context (Dobash et al. 1992; Kimmel 2002). For example, the CTS does not distinguish a wife hitting her husband out of anger and frustration from a wife who attacks her husband to prevent him from harming their children. Second, the family conflict surveys employed by Straus (e.g., 1990; Straus and Gelles 1990) interviewed only couples that were *currently* involved. Former spouses, boyfriends, and girlfriends were not included, and former intimate partners might be more motivated to engage in violence (Kimmel 2002; DeKeseredy et al. 2006). Third, family conflict surveys do not include sexual assaults and rape, criminal events which account for a significant proportion of intimate partner violence.

The fourth common criticism of family conflict surveys and the CTS concerns the conclusions that have been drawn from these surveys (i.e., that women are equally capable of violence). Proponents of gender symmetry focus only on the prevalence of partner abuse *perpetration* by men and women to draw their conclusions of symmetry (Johnson 2010), and they do not take into account the consequences of the violence. Women are much more likely than men to sustain injuries as a result of IPV. This finding is the one thing that proponents and opponents of the gender symmetry debate agree upon (Dobash et al. 1992; Kimmel 2002; Straus 1997, 1999). According to some reports, women are six times more likely than men to sustain serious injuries that require medical attention at the hands of an intimate partner (Kaufman and Straus 1987; Stets and Straus 1990). Based on the family conflict studies, the injury rate for male-to-female partner assaults is about seven times greater than the injury rate for female-to-male partner assaults (Straus 1997; Stets and Straus 1990).

The final common criticism of data used by gender symmetry proponents is the high refusal rate of the NFVS, which is 40% (Johnson 2010). A non-response rate that high undermines the representativeness of this survey. It is possible that men who perpetrate serious violence against their wives (intimate terrorists, described below) would decline to participate in these surveys because they do not want to incriminate themselves; their abused wives might not want to participate in these surveys because they fear retribution from their abusive husbands. Opponents of the gender symmetry perspective have relied on crime victimization surveys, which consist mostly of large-scale surveys funded and administered by government agencies (Kimmel 2002). Most such surveys include a wide range of victimizations by current and former significant others. The NVAW survey (described above, Tjaden and Thoennes 1998, 2000) and the NCVS are the two most popular crime victimization surveys. The NCVS, administered by the Bureau of Justice Statistics, surveys more than 76,000 households and 135,000 individuals age 12 and older annually about the "frequency, characteristics and consequences of criminal victimization in the United States" (Bureau of Justice Statistics 2008). Opponents of gender symmetry also rely on data from court and police records, calls to 911, stays at shelters, and emergency room visits.

Studies that have relied on official sources of data and crime victimization surveys overwhelmingly have found gender asymmetry in couple violence (Kimmel 2002). Data from the 1992-1993 NCVS revealed that, compared to men, women reported six times more incidents of violent victimizations by intimate partners (Bachman and Saltzman 1995; Dawson and Langan 1994). The 1998 NVAW survey found that, compared to women, men assaulted their partners three times more often (Tjaden and Thoennes 2000).

In contrast to family conflict studies, crime victimization surveys (with the exception of the NCVS) have also found a much lower prevalence of domestic assaults. Rates of couple violence are around 1% of all couples per year based on crime victimization surveys and 16% a year based on family conflict studies (Kimmel 2002; Straus 1990, 1999). The lower prevalence rate in data that are drawn from crime victimization surveys, calls to the police, emergency room visits, and women's shelters is likely due to the fact that they capture only serious domestic assaults that require police and/or medical attention. When less serious forms of violence are excluded from the data, yearly prevalence rate is reduced to around 6% of all couples (Kimmel 2002; Straus and Gelles 1986).

This, according to proponents of gender symmetry, is the principal problem with relying on data from emergency services; these data capture only the most serious episodes of domestic violence. According to Straus (1999) these serious episodes of violence represent only a fraction of all intimate partner violence. Family conflict surveys include many minor incidents of violence that are not typically reported to authorities and that do not typically result in injury. Thus, the different sources of data could explain the overwhelming *symmetry* found in family conflict surveys and *asymmetry* found in data from crime victimization surveys and official sources of data.

Intimate Terrorism, Violent Resistance, and Situational Couple Violence

Johnson (1995, 2008; Johnson and Ferraro 2000) has argued that both sides of the debate are at least partially correct, because each is describing a different type of intimate partner violence. According to Johnson (2008, 2), "there is more than one type of intimate partner violence: some studies address the type of violence perpetrated primarily by men, while others are getting at the kind of violence that women are involved in as well." Following this argument, Johnson proposed the following four types of intimate partner violence, which are distinguished by the extent to which general control is the motive for the violence: intimate terrorism (IT), violent resistance (VR), situational couple violence (SCV), and mutual violent control (MVC). The three most common types of IPV (and the three types of violence that are the center of the debate outlined above) are IT, VR, and SCV.

When people use the phrase "domestic violence," IT is probably what they have in mind (Johnson 2008). Intimate terrorism is the type of violence that receives the most media attention and it was and is the focus of the battered women's movement. This type of partner abuse involves an abuser controlling his or her partner with continued violence, along with intimidation, isolation, economic control, and other psychological tactics of oppression. Perpetrators of IT are almost always male, although there are some instances among heterosexual couples of women terrorizing male partners. Johnson (2008) estimated that more than two million women are victims of IT in the U.S. each year. Among IT, VR, and SCV, IT is most likely to result in serious injury for female victims. The pattern of power and control exhibited in

IT is very similar to Stark's (2007) coercive control and the pattern of violence described by Pence and Paymar (1993).

According to Pence and Paymar (1993), perpetrators of intimate terrorism often use intimidation techniques to control their partners through overt displays of rage (e.g., screaming, smashing things, killing beloved pets). Many abusers also assume complete economic control, requiring their wives to hand over paychecks and demanding that they account for every penny spent. A single instance of intimidation, economic control, or violence does not constitute IT. Rather, IT is a pattern of serious abuse and control committed over an extended period of time.

Violent resistance occurs when a victim of intimate terrorism fights back or defends herself (Johnson 2008). The key elements that distinguish VR from other types of IPV are the motive for her violence, the violence of her partner, and the motive for her partner's violence. A female who commits VR is the victim of intimate terrorism; her violence is not motivated by the need to control her partner, but her partner's violence is motivated by the desire to control her. Violent resistance is almost always committed by females against male partners, and it is fleeting, given the male's ability to physically dominate the female. Females who resort to violence to cope with their partners' violence usually resort to other methods of coping, including denial, depression, escaping, and in rare cases, homicide.

Situational couple violence, the most common type of partner abuse, occurs when an argument, often one incident, escalates to violence (Johnson 2008). Instances of SCV can occur only once, can be sporadic, or can be frequent. The severity of SCV can range from a benign slap across the face to a beating that requires medical attention; in extreme cases it can result in homicide.

The motives behind SCV can vary. The motive behind an instance of violence could be to express extreme rage, or it could be control (e.g., to gain compliance). In fact, a single occurrence of SCV and IT may be indistinguishable to an observer. What separates the two types of violence is the pattern of control and violence surrounding the violence. Intimate terrorism is part of a pattern of control, while SCV is not part of a long-standing attempt to completely control the partner. Results from a study by Graham-Kevan and Archer (2005) provided support for the existence of this type of couple violence. The authors found that when women from the study took part in mutual aggression, they were provoked more by their partner's violence (SCV) than by fear (VR) or the need to control their partners (IT). Another characteristic that distinguishes SCV from IT is that males and females are just as likely to initiate this type of violence. However, when males initiate the violence, they are much more likely to cause injury and introduce fear and intimidation into the relationship.

The purpose of including Johnson's (2008) typology of IPV in this research, and making a distinction between mutual and one-sided violence in the data, is to demonstrate that some forms of IPV are similar to general violent victimization while other forms of IPV are different from general violence and should be understood separately. Situational couple violence, for example, likely follows a pattern similar to that of general violence. For example, in SCV the violence witnessed arises out of arguments that have escalated out of control, as often occurs with general violence. Intimate terrorism, on the other hand, is not sporadic and often involves psychological abuse, unlike general violence. The victims are usually female, the violence is an expression of patriarchy and misogyny, and each instance of violence is generally unprovoked. Each of these types of IPV is likely to have different risk factors and to be associated with different deviant behaviors.

Adolescent Intimate Partner Violence

Because scholarly research on adolescent romantic relationships and the recognition of teen dating violence as a serious problem are only relatively recent developments (Collins 2003), most of the theory and research on adolescent IPV is based on observations and research on adult relationships (Mulford and Giordano 2008). This *lacuna* limits our understanding of teen dating violence because the adult domestic violence framework might not be useful for understanding teen dating violence, given the known dissimilarities between adult and adolescent relationships.

Adolescent relationships are different from adult relationships because most of these young partnerships lack economic dependence and parenthood, factors which are more common in adulthood. Without these elements, adolescent relationships are more transitory, and the participants are less invested and emotionally involved than their adult counterparts. Thus, the same factors that can explain conflict within adult relationships (e.g., economic hardship, the stress of parenthood) are not applicable to adolescent relationships. Adolescent romantic involvement can be quite distinct from adult partnerships, given the novelty of these unions for the participants and the heightened social awkwardness that often accompanies them.

Theoretically, adult partner abuse is often explained by male patriarchy, social learning (e.g., family history of aggression, cultural influence), and evolutionary psychology. Feminists argue that heterosexual relationships are embedded in male-dominated societies, and the cultural dominance of males can seep into personal relationships (Dobash and Dobash 1992). Patriarchy motivates males to exert dominance and control over their female partners, and sometimes dominance comes in the form of controlling behaviors and violence.

Many sociologists and social psychologists assert that early exposure to families and cultures in which control and violence are common elements of relationships can result in the re-creation of these behaviors into adulthood (Archer 2006; Busby, Holman, and Walker 2008). Social learning theories, favored by sociologists, posit that people learn both deviant and conforming behaviors through close contacts with families, friends, and other significant individuals (Burgess and Akers 1966; Sutherland and Cressey 1955). If adolescents witness IPV or misogyny in their homes and cultures, they are likely to adopt these behaviors if the following things happen: (a) they learn the practical aspects of engaging in IPV (e.g., how and why); (b) they observe that this behavior (IPV) is rewarded or at least not punished; and, (c) they successfully imitate this behavior (Akers et al. 1979). People become abusers, or perhaps victims through social interactions with others who engage in IPV (as victims or abusers), through which they learn attitudes and motivations that are conducive to IPV.

Evolutionary psychologists argue that both males and females are motivated by feelings of jealousy, which may lead to IPV (Kaighobadi, Shackelford, and Goetz 2009). Both genders are instinctively concerned with the fidelity of their romantic partners. Males are particularly concerned with certainty about paternity, whereas females are concerned with emotional fidelity. Exclusively monogamous relationships can ensure both of these goals. For males especially, jealousy and uncertainty about monogamy can motivate controlling behaviors, which can take the form of verbal abuse, sexual coercion, and physical violence. Based on this theory, the risk of male-perpetrated IPV should be a function of the female's reproductive value (Peters, Shackelford, and Buss 2002). In support of this proposition, Peters et al. (2002) found that younger women are at the greatest risk of IPV victimization, and that the risk of IPV victimization for females decreases with age (as they become less fertile). Likewise, younger men who are also better able to reproduce compared to their older counterparts, are likely to perpetrate IPV.

Although these explanations are more often used to explain adult partner abuse, some of these explanations may also apply to adolescent relationship violence. As described earlier, adolescent romantic relationships are different from adult romantic relationships in some key ways. However, adolescent relationships also carry many of the same qualities that make adult relationships/marriages satisfying, including elements of commitment, emotional support, passion, and feelings of "togetherness" (Levesque 1993).

Patriarchy is an example of an otherwise useful theoretical perspective that is not very useful for understanding adolescent IPV. Evidence suggests that adolescent relationships are more equal than adult relationships because traditional sex roles of male dominance and female dependence have not taken yet hold (Mulford and Giordano 2008; Wekerle and Wolfe 1999). Giordano's (2007) study of 7th, 9th, and 11th graders in Toledo revealed that most adolescents report equal power in romantic relationships, with girls tending to take the upper hand in imbalanced relationships (Mulford and Giordano 2008).

Social learning and cultural explanations of partner abuse, on the other hand, are useful for understanding teen dating violence. By studying the influence of families (Matsueda and Heimer 1987) and peer networks (Warr 2002) on adolescent offending and drug use, criminologists have established that young people often learn deviant behaviors from personal contacts. Thus, it is possible that witnessing IPV among family members and peer groups can lead to conflict within an adolescent's own relationships. Evolutionary psychology may also be useful for understanding teen partner abuse. Even in the absence of economic strain and parenthood, feelings of jealousy over sexual and emotional infidelity may still be present in adolescent romantic relationships. Also, many adolescents are entering their prime reproductive years, which can increase the likelihood of male-perpetrated IPV (Peters et al. 2002).

Prior Research on Adolescent IPV

Several studies on the prevalence and consequences of teen dating abuse have emerged over the past decade (e.g., Ackard et al. 2007; Coker et al. 2000; Eaton et al. 2007; Halpern et al. 2001; Olshen et al. 2007). Using a sample of about 7,000 male and female adolescents from the Add Health data, Halpern et al. (2001) found that a little over 5,000 of the respondents had been involved in at least one romantic relationship in the previous 18 months. Roughly one third of the respondents who were involved in romantic relationships reported some type of partner abuse, ranging from being cursed at to being shoved and having something thrown at them. Ten percent of the respondents experienced physical abuse, a figure that is consistent with the report from the CDC (National Center for Injury Prevention 2006).

The results from the Halpern et al. (2001) study also indicated that involvement in more than one romantic relationship increased the odds of victimization. Other correlates of adolescent IPV varied by sex. The odds of physical and psychological abuse for adolescent males were higher for non-whites, boys from non-traditional households, and sons of less-educated parents. The odds of psychological abuse were higher for females from single-father homes and less religious families. Grade point average was negatively associated with both physical and psychological abuse only for females.

Another noteworthy finding from the Halpern et al. (2001) study was that males and females reported nearly identical rates of victimization for nearly all types of abuse. This finding has been replicated in several other studies of adolescents (e.g., Capaldi, Kim, and Shortt 2007; Giordano 2007; Jezl, Molidor, and Wright 1996; O'Leary et al. 2008; O'Keefe 1997). For example, Giordano's (2007) survey of 7th, 9th, and 11th graders revealed that nearly 50% of the males and more than half of the females in abusive relationships reported that the violence was mutual (Mulford and Giordano 2008). A much larger proportion of the females reported that they were the sole aggressors of the abuse (30% of females versus 6% of males). Nearly half of the males reported that they were the sole victims of the aggression. Using a modified version of the CTS, O'Leary et al. (2007) found that from a sample of more than 2,000 high school students in New York more females reported aggression towards their partners (40%) than victimization by their male partners (30%). Data from the males complements this finding, with 24% reporting aggression and 31% reporting victimization. Further evidence from this study suggested that relationship violence mostly involved mutual aggression.

Although adolescent romantic relationships are different from adult romantic relationships in some key ways, studies of adolescent IPV have revealed four patterns that are consistent with adult IPV. First, it appears that surveys using the CTS administered to adolescents also reveal some evidence of gender symmetry (just as this survey instrument does for adults). Second, rates of serious injuries are much higher for female than male victims (Gray and Foshee 1997; Malik, Sorenson, and Aneshensel 1997; Morse 1995). Third, in addition to more severe physical injuries, adolescent girls also suffer more long-term health problems, including impaired mental health and substance abuse problems (Ackard et al. 2007; Olshen et al. 2007). Fourth, at least one study has found that females are more likely to engage in violence in self-defense. O'Keefe's (1997) study of dating violence among high school students found that although anger motivated most of the violence for boys and girls, girls were more likely than boys to report self-defense as the motive for their violence and boys were more likely than girls to report control.

To date, Johnson's (2008) typology of abuse has not been applied to research on the causes and correlates of adolescent IPV. The present study will include an approximation of Johnson's typology in part of the analyses. Although Mulford and Giordano (2008) argued that adult theories of intimate partner violence are not useful for understanding teen dating violence, Johnson's framework might be applicable to adolescents given that similar patterns of adolescent and adult IPV victimization have been established (e.g., comparable rates of male and female victimization and more injurious female victimization).

Johnson and Ferraro (2000) asserted that scholars cannot assume that all partner abuse is the same. A mutually aggressive abusive relationship is quite distinct from a relationship in which one partner terrorizes the other. The causes and correlates of different types of IPV likely vary among adults (Johnson 2010; Macmillan and Gartner 1999), and they likely do among adolescents as well. For example, regarding the risk factors for IPV victimization among adolescents, a history of delinquency and violent offending is probably less predictive of being victimized by one-sided partner abuse (intimate terrorism) than of being involved in a mutually violent relationship. In other words, adolescents with a history of violent offending and delinquency may self-select into tumultuous partnerships that are characterized by violence. Adolescents who have a history of violent victimization, on the other hand, are probably more likely to become the victims of one-sided IPV because of the stability in victimization over time (Schreck, Stewart, and Fisher 2006; Wittebrood and Nieuwbeerta 2000).

Correlates of Adolescent IPV

Teen dating violence has been linked with several negative behaviors. Using a longitudinal sample of more than 1,500 male and female adolescents, Ackard et al. (2007) found that for female victims teen dating violence was significantly correlated with tobacco and marijuana use and with depression. Several other studies have correlated dating violence with poor physical and mental health among females (Coker et al. 2000; Campbell 2002; Olshen et al. 2007). Among a sample of more than 4,000 high school girls, Silverman et al. (2001) found that victims of dating violence (both physical and sexual abuse) experienced an increased risk of substance use, eating disorders, suicidal ideation, and risky sexual behavior. Eaton and colleagues (2007) also found an association between teen dating violence and risky sexual behavior. Based on a study of more than 600 high school boys and girls, Bergman (1992) found that teen dating violence was associated with a lower grade-point average, although school performance is also thought to be a risk factor for dating violence (Halpern et al. 2001).

Dating violence is also associated with minor delinquency (Roberts, Klein, and Fisher 2003). Based on two waves of the Add Health data, Roberts et al. found that the dating violence that occurred between the first and second waves of data was associated with substance use, delinquency, violent behavior, and diminished mental health.

Effects of General Victimization

The above findings parallel research on the outcomes of non-relationship victimization, which is more common among adolescents than other age groups (Catalano 2006). Adolescents and young adults experience the highest rates of victimization for most types of crime, and especially for violent crime. Individuals ranging in age from 12 to 15-years-old have the highest rates of violent victimization, followed closely by individuals 16 to 24-years-old (47 and 45 victimizations per 1,000 persons, respectively; Catalano 2006). Rates of violent victimization drop by almost half by the time individuals reach the age of 25.

Given the risk of violent victimization and the timing and importance of adolescence in the life course for long-term development, criminologists have developed a large body of research dedicated to the short and long-term effects of adolescent victimization (Macmillan 2001). For both adolescents and adults the experience of violent victimization is associated with poor health, self-destructive behaviors, and deviant behaviors, although this relationship is stronger for adolescents (Menard 2002). Non-relationship victimization is also associated with mental health problems, drug and alcohol use, and criminal offending (Hindelang, Gottfredson, and Garofalo 1978; Menard 2002; Resick and Nishith 1997; Sampson and Lauritsen 1990).

Research has shown that adolescent victims and adolescent offenders are often the same people (Lauritsen, Sampson, and Laub 1991; Shaffer and Ruback 2002). Sometimes these individuals alternate between offending and victimization. Although some research has identified pure victims and pure offenders, these groups are relatively small (Schreck, Stewart, and Osgood 2008).

Past research on teen dating violence has not acknowledged the potential for a reciprocal relationship between victimization and offending (including substance use, general delinquency, and violent behavior). Most researchers of teen dating violence view victims as passive targets of abuse. These researchers do not consider deviant behavior as a risk factor for teen dating violence; they view it only as a potential outcome. Given that a large proportion of teen dating violence appears to be mutually perpetrated, this omission leaves the literature with an incomplete picture of this type of victimization. Adolescent IPV may have a direct effect on deviant outcomes, such as delinquency and drug use. However, past occurrences of these behaviors may predict both the victimization and influence these deviant outcomes.

Not only is offending a risk factor for victimization, but victimization is also associated with offending in adulthood (Macmillan

2001; Menard 2002). Child abuse victimization is associated with criminal behavior in adulthood (Grogan-Kaylor and Otis 2003; Widom 1989) as well as dating violence (Reuterman and Burcky 1989; Roscoe and Callahan 1985). Non-family adolescent victimization is also related to criminal behavior in adulthood (Fagan, Piper, and Cheng 1987), and victims of adolescent violence are also more likely to engage in domestic violence in adulthood, both as victims and perpetrators (Menard 2002). According to Menard's (2002) analysis of the National Youth Survey, victims of violence during adolescence are also likely to be victims of violence during adulthood, apart from relationship violence.

In the short-term, victims of crime, and especially victims of violent crime, experience diminished physical and mental health (e.g., Klaus 1994; Lurigio 1987; Norris, Kaniasty, and Thompson 1997; Resick and Nishith 1997). Several studies have also linked adolescent victimization to psychological problems in adulthood (for a review, see Macmillan 2001), and this is equally true for parental abuse (Briere and Runtz 1988; Chu and Dill 1990), sexual assault (Burnam et al. 1998), and physical assault (Duncan et al. 1996). Post-traumatic stress disorder is commonly linked with adolescent victimization (Menard 2002).

Victims of crime also incur financial losses related directly and indirectly to the victimization (Miller, Cohen, and Wiersema 1996). Direct financial costs include losses related to the victimization, medical costs related to injury, and costs associated with psychological trauma (Macmillan 2000). Indirect costs include loss of wages and productivity because victims of crime often miss days of work (Perkins et al. 1996; Miller et al. 1996). Adolescent victimization also affects wages and productivity into adulthood by disrupting educational attainment, which leads to lower wages (Macmillan 2000). According to Macmillan, victimization that occurs during adolescence is associated with the largest losses.

Clearly, adolescent victimization is related to poor health and deviant behaviors. However, the mechanisms that link adolescent victimization to poor health and deviance in adulthood are less clear. Macmillan and Hagan (2004) found that adolescent victimization often sets off a chain reaction in which victimization affects educational achievement and psychological well-being, which in turn affects socioeconomic status in adulthood, which in turn can have several other negative effects. Besides disrupting educational attainment and mental health, early victimization may also result in repeat victimization, which could in turn have wide-ranging effects on socioeconomic attainment and offending in adulthood (Menard and Huizinga 2001).

Limitations of the Research on Adolescent Intimate Partner Violence

The research on adolescent intimate partner violence suffers from three major limitations. First, many of the studies cited were limited to cross-sectional data. Without longitudinal data, researchers cannot determine the timing of abuse relative to other negative outcomes. Controlling for prior victimization or offending is important, given the overlap between victimization and offending outlined above. Further, without longitudinal data, the researchers cannot take into account prior behavioral problems. Given that the best predictor of future behavior is past behavior, pre-existing behavioral problems may account for much of the relationship between intimate partner violence and negative outcomes. Past behaviors, such as delinquency and violence, may also be risk factors for intimate partner violence.

Second, many of the samples underlying the studies cited were limited to adolescent females. Because rates of male and female IPV victimization are similar (Halpern et al. 2001; O'Keefe 1997), and couple violence is often mutual (Mulford and Giordano 2008), it is important to include males and females in an effort to include all victims and to take different types of couple violence into account (i.e., mutual violence versus one-sided violence). The correlates and consequences of IPV may also vary by gender.

Finally, there is a lack of research on adolescent intimate partner violence that takes into account the influence of peer networks. Peer influence is more prominent during adolescence than during any other time (Giordano, Cernkovich, and Pugh 1986). Peers influence delinquent behavior (Haynie 2002), and more recent research suggests that the attitudes of peers can influence how adolescents react to dating violence (Adelman and Kil 2007). Given the importance of friendships during adolescence, it is necessary to examine how peers influence this type of victimization.

The Add Health data make it possible to address these three limitations. The longitudinal design of Add Health allows this project to control for early delinquency and to examine partner abuse over time. Further, the Add Health study includes detailed information on peer networks allowing for an investigation of how peers influence IPV (e.g., the mean delinquency and violence among peer networks, the size and density of a peer network). Moreover, the secure romantic partnership portion of these data allow researchers to link couples. Accessing these secure data allows the present study to identify couples in which only one partner reports victimization versus couples in which both partners report victimization.

Ideally, this study would be able to identify three most common types of IPV identified by Johnson (SCV, VR, and IT). However, the data allow only for a distinction between aggression initiated by one or both partners, and it cannot establish the motivations for the abuse. Aggression initiated by only one partner could be either violent resistance or it could be intimate terrorism. Further, aggression initiated by both partners could be SCV, or it could be IT by one partner and VR by the other. Thus, this study is not able to fully apply Johnson's typology to adolescents. However, this study represents the first step towards doing so.

The Role of Peer Groups in Offending and Victimization

Any examination of adolescent offending or victimization should take into account peer influence. Friendships are central in the lives of adolescents, as they begin to establish independence and spend more time away from their parents (Giordano et al. 1986). Adolescents spend equal, if not more, time with their peers as compared to parents (Brown 1982; Montemayor 1982), and they spend a sizeable proportion of their free time socializing with peers (Larson and Kleiber 1993).

Besides the rising importance of peers, another hallmark of adolescence is exposure to delinquent peers (Warr 1993). This exposure is important to consider because it can influence individual offending (Warr and Stafford 1991; Haynie 2001; Haynie 2002). Exposure to delinquent peers increases through the early teen years, peaks during the middle and late teen years, and declines into early adulthood (Warr 1998, 2002). In fact, exposure to delinquent peers can at least partially explain the age-crime curve because exposure to delinquent peers corresponds with rates of offending among adolescents and young adults. Warr (1998) found that major life course transitions, such as marriage, were linked to a decrease in the number of deviant peers and the time spent with those peers, which in turn explained decreases in offending.

There are two characteristics of delinquent peer interactions that can explain individual offending. First is the number of delinquent peers. Most adolescents have at least a few delinquent peers (Haynie 2001). In other words, few friendship networks are completely devoid of any delinquent peer interactions. However, the more delinquent peers an individual has, and the more delinquency those peers engage in, the more likely the individual is to engage in delinquency (Warr and Stafford. 1991). The effect of associating with delinquent peers is often the strongest predictor of individual offending in criminological studies (Akers et al. 1979; Warr and Stafford 1991).

The second major attribute of delinquent peer associations that can explain individual offending is the structural characteristics of the peer networks. Haynie (2001) found that large and more cohesive friendship networks have more influence on delinquent behavior than smaller loosely coupled networks. Also, peer networks that are intimate in nature and whose members frequently interact have great influence on the behavior of individuals (Agnew 1991). Female friendship networks tend to be more cohesive and their members are more conforming, which could partially explain why females engage in less deviant behavior compared to males (Broidy and Agnew 1997).

The mechanisms that explain the relationship between peer delinquency and individual offending have not been fully articulated. However, several scholars have argued that delinquent peers influence individual offending through a learning process in which delinquent peers teach individuals how and why to engage in criminal behavior criminal behavior (Agnew 1991; Akers et al. 1979; Sutherland and Cressey 1955). This perspective is guided by social learning theory, and it is discussed in greater detail in Chapter 2. Also, the direction of this causal relationship is not clear. In other words, delinquent peers may not necessarily influence individual offending, but rather a delinquent individual may seek out delinquent peers.

In addition to influencing delinquent behavior, peers can also influence the likelihood of victimization (Schreck and Fisher 2004; Schreck, Miller, and Gibson 2003). Schreck et al. (2003) found that individuals who had central roles in dense conforming peer networks were less likely to be victimized, while individuals with central roles in densely populated delinquent peer groups were more likely to be victimized. Schreck and Fisher's (2004) study of families, peer networks, and victimization revealed that loose attachment to family and exposure to delinquent peer groups were both associated with a rise in the likelihood of victimization, even after controlling for limited supervision, unstructured socializing, and several other relevant factors. Delinquent peers probably influence the likelihood of victimization because this exposure represents exposure to risk. Being in close proximity to deviant others has obvious implications for victimization, either by the deviant peers or by others provoked by the deviant peers.

Because having deviant peers influences the risk of both offending and victimization, it is reasonable to expect that deviant peers can influence the likelihood of IPV victimization and influence deviant behaviors associated with IPV victimization. Having delinquent and, especially, violent peers could increase the risk of IPV victimization because adolescents are likely to select their romantic partners from their friendship circles. Deviant romantic partners are more likely to engage in partner abuse.

The structural characteristics of the peer networks could also influence the risk of IPV victimization. More popular adolescents are probably less likely to experience IPV victimization because close peers could act as "capable guardians" in the words of Cohen and Felson (1979; this phenomenon is explained in more detail in Chapter 2). These peers could both recognize and intervene in abusive relationships. In contrast, individuals with few or no close friends might make ideal targets for IPV victimization because these isolated adolescents have little protection.

A large peer group could also ward off would-be abusive romantic partners. Potential abusers could perceive that a large supportive peer group would not tolerate the abuse of one of its members. Large supportive peer groups also provide social and emotional support and raise the self-esteem of their members, both of which are negatively associated with personal victimization (Hodges and Perry 1999). A large supportive and conforming peer group could also influence how an adolescent reacts to IPV victimization. Supportive peer groups would likely encourage healthy coping mechanisms to deal with IPV victimization. In contrast, because adolescents embedded in deviant peer groups are probably already likely to engage in deviant behavior, it is reasonable to expect that they will engage in more deviance in response to IPV victimization.

Even though popularity could decrease one's risk of victimization, more popular teens are probably more likely to date compared to less popular teens. Their involvement in multiple romantic relationships probably increases their risk of IPV victimization (Halpern et al. 2001). By contrast, less popular adolescents are less likely to date, and as a result are less likely to be victimized by romantic partners.

Gendered and Violence Perspectives on IPV

The overall objective of this research is to determine the extent to which adolescent IPV is similar to other forms of violent behavior as opposed to being distinct from general violence. Does IPV follow other patterns of violence, in which certain individuals are more prone to victimization as a result of violent offending and other imprudent behaviors (e.g., illicit drug use)? Are these behaviors predictive of one another, just as general violent offending and violent victimization are (Shaffer and Ruback 2002)? Is victimization by an intimate partner predictive of general violent offending, delinquency, and drug use, net of prior behaviors?

There are two general approaches to IPV research. The first approach, alluded to in an earlier section of this chapter, is rooted in a feminist perspective and is referred to as the "gender perspective" by Felson (2006; Felson and Lane 2010). Many feminist IPV researchers (e.g., DeKeseredy and Kelly 1993; Dobash and Dobash 1979) argue that men who use violence against their wives are motivated by misogyny and the desire to control their partners. The desire of men to control women is influenced by the patriarchal society in which these relationships are embedded, which teaches men the value of exerting dominance over women. Sometimes, this exertion of dominance takes the form of violence. When women use violence against their male partners, they are likely defending themselves from the violence of their male partners.

The second main approach to IPV research is the "violence perspective" (Felson 2006; Felson and Lane 2010), which emphasizes the similarities of IPV to more general forms of violence (e.g., non-partner related assaults). In other words, according to this view, even though general violent victimization and IPV victimization are often studied as two distinct phenomena, IPV is not a unique class of violence. Partner abuse is the result of motivations and circumstances similar to those causing general violence and can be understood in the same way as other forms of violent behavior. Thus, the study of IPV as a distinct brand of violence is misguided. According to Felson (2002, 16), "all aggression is instrumental," and we use aggression as a means to various ends.

Felson's (2002) violence approach holds that violence is coercive aggression intended to harm another person. The purpose of violence could be to protect one's social identity, to achieve justice, or to gain compliance from another individual. Sometimes the violence is used against a target who in some way provoked the aggressor (dispute-related), and sometimes the violence is directed at a target who is not immediately involved with the situation (predatory). Consider the following example: a husband thinks that he is being treated unfairly at work, and as a result of this treatment he physically abuses his wife when he gets home. Following Felson's perspective on violence, the violence described in this example is predatory violence that is motivated by justice. The same description could be applied to a situation in which the husband abuses one of his children, or if this same husband went to a bar after work and, unprovoked, hit another bar patron.

Feminist domestic violence scholars would argue that the violence in the first example was motivated by sexism or misogyny. Felson (2002) does not deny that extreme patriarchy or misogyny provokes *some* instances of violence. Rather, Felson asserts that there is not an epidemic of IPV, and these motivations do not explain a unique class of violence.

Feminist scholars argue that IPV is a unique form of violence because the motivations for the violence are distinct and the victims are usually female. Young, African American, unmarried men are more often the victims of general violence, and this phenomenon is often explained by the routine activities in which they engage (Hindelang et al. 1978; Lauritsen et al. 1991). Individuals who spend more time outside of the home, late at night, and in places that are vulnerable to violence are more likely to become victims of violence. Delinquency and offending behaviors also place individuals at risk for violence. This demographic group (young, African American, and/or unmarried) are more likely to engage in all of these behaviors. Thus, when women, and especially married women, become the victims of violence, these occurrences are unique and should be examined separately. Given that all women, specifically married or cohabiting women, engage in fewer activities that place them at risk for violence, the explanations and motivations for this type of violence must be different.

The gender and violence perspectives on IPV can be partially reconciled, and that is one of the goals of this research. Johnson (2008) argued that there are multiple types of IPV, which are likely distinct in their origins and consequences (Johnson 1995; Johnson 2010). Some forms of IPV can be explained by traditional feminist explanations (e.g., patriarchy, control, misogyny), and some instances of IPV are similar to other general forms of violence.

Intimate terrorism and mutual violent control are both part of larger patterns of violence or psychological terrorism that can be explained by the desire to control and dominate a partner. Because intimate terrorism is usually perpetrated by males against their female partners, this type of violence is probably more explainable with feminist theories of IPV. Situational couple violence is less likely to be part of a larger pattern of control and violence. It is commonly perpetrated by both males and females within relationships, and it tends to be less serious (although it could result in serious injury or homicide). These instances of violence are often dispute-related and motivated by the desire to achieve compliance or "save face." This type of violence is consistent with the arguments made by Felson (2006). Thus, some forms of IPV are consistent with feminist theories of IPV (the former), while other forms of IPV are consistent with Felson's perspective of violence (the latter).

Gender, Crime, and Victimization

Given that most studies of IPV are limited to female samples, another major goal of this research is to include both male and female adolescents in order to compare the causes and correlates of IPV victimization for both groups. Gender plays a central role in both general violence and IPV. Men are commonly the perpetrators and victims of one type of violence (general violence), while women are commonly the victims and sometimes the perpetrators of the other

(IPV). Gender is often used to explain these disparities. For example, opportunity theorists explain the higher rates of male victimization by non-partner-related violence by the fact that men spend more time in situations that are conducive to violence. Felson (1996) would argue that females perpetrate IPV less often than men because they are, on average, smaller than men. Thus, in a study that integrates research on two gendered phenomena (i.e., general violence and IPV), it is important to consider the role of gender.

Compared to males, females occupy a much smaller role in criminal offending and violent behavior. Adolescent females account for only 30% of all juvenile arrests, and an even smaller proportion of arrests for violent crime (Zahn et al. 2010). Juvenile arrests for violent crime have been mostly declining since 1994, but the rate of change has varied for boys and girls. Arrests for aggravated assault decreased by 24% for boys, but only 10% for girls. Additionally, arrests for simple assault decreased by 4% for boys while they increased by 19% for girls. Arrest rates for adolescent males and females, which have historically been lopsided with many more male arrests, may be starting to converge. However, arrest data may be misleading. Changes in arrest rates may simply reflect changes in enforcement and detection strategies rather than actual changes in behavior.

When females do engage in criminal and violent behavior, there is some evidence that the same social forces that explain male behavior also explain female behavior (Mazerolle 1998; Miller 1998; Miller 2001; Steffensmeier and Allan 1996). For example, risky behaviors and delinquency are associated with stressors or traumatic life events, including abusive home environments, for both adolescent males and females (McBurnett et al. 2005; Sinha 2000; Zahn et al. 2010). Based on a review of more than 1,600 studies on juvenile delinquency, Zahn and colleagues (2010) concluded that factors such as economic disadvantage, poor parental attachment and supervision, childhood abuse, and exposure to violence influence both male and female delinquency.

Besides frequency, there are some key differences in types of delinquency between male and female adolescent offending. First, early puberty seems to affect males and females differently. For adolescent females, early puberty is a particularly strong risk factor for substance use, running away from home, and truancy (Caspi and Moffitt 1991;

Zahn et al. 2010). Early-maturing females are more likely to interact with older males compared to their less developed counterparts, and interactions with older males can lead to deviant behavior and offending. Early puberty is also tied to conflict with parents (Moffitt et al. 1992). The interaction between early puberty, frequent interactions with older male peers, and loose parental attachment is strongly related to female delinquency and less so for male delinquency.

Most adolescent female offending comprises less serious offenses, including running away from home and truancy (Daly and Chesney-Lind 1988; Zahn et al. 2010). These behaviors are often motivated by victimization. Studies of female runaways have revealed that this behavior is highly correlated with sexual and physical victimization (e.g., Feitel et al. 1992; Stiffman 1989; Zahn et al. 2010). Thus, adolescent female victimization can lead to minor deviant acts that can leave females vulnerable to subsequent victimization.

Miller's (2001) ethnographic study of male and female gang members provides an example of the strong relationship between prior victimization and offending. Miller (2001) found that although both male and female gang members came principally from disadvantaged environments and broken homes, the female gang members differed from male gang members in four ways. First, the female gang members were more likely to come from abusive homes, including physical, emotional, and sexual abuse. Second, once the females were in the gangs, they experienced more victimization, usually at the hands of fellow male gang members (including romantic partners). Third, female gang members were more likely to engage in criminal activity and violent offending than females outside of gangs. However, they still engaged in much less criminal and violent behavior than male gang members. Lastly, female gang members were much less likely than male gang members to be in leadership roles within the gangs.

Mazerolle (1998) also found some similarities and differences in adolescent male and female offending. In a test of Agnew's General Strain Theory, Mazerolle found that males and females were susceptible to the same types of strain (e.g., negative relations with adults, negative life events). Males and females differed, however, in how they responded to strain. Males were inclined to express anger and engage in violent offending against others while females were more likely to engage in self-destructive behaviors.

Based on the criminology literature, there are three likely gender differences in the relationship between general violent victimization, violent offending, and IPV victimization over time. First, prior violent victimization should be more predictive of IPV for females than for males. Based on the study by Miller (2001), it appears that there is more consistency in victimization for females over time. The female gang members interviewed by Miller were more likely to have been victimized in their homes, followed by more victimization as gang members. This expected relationship is also consistent with Simons et al. (1993), who found that females subjected to harsh parenting as children were more likely to develop aggressive and deviant behaviors as adults, and they were more likely to be assaulted by their spouses/partners. The authors explained the relationship between childhood maltreatment, offending, and IPV victimization with assortative mating. That is, women who become aggressive and deviant as a result of harsh parenting are more likely to associate with and select their partners from networks of aggressive and deviant men.

Second, males and females experience different consequences as a result of experiencing victimization. Victimization by an intimate partner should be more predictive of an increase in violent offending for males than for females. Following Mazerolle's (1998) study, IPV victimization could represent a form of strain, and males appear to be likely to react to strain with anger and violence more so than females. Thus, females should be expected to react with more self-destructive behaviors, such as drug and alcohol use, risky sexual behaviors, and suicidal ideation. This finding would be consistent with other research on IPV victimization and adverse outcomes (Campbell 2002; Coker et al. 2000; Olshen et al. 2007).

The third major difference between males and females concerns how peer network characteristics influence the relationships between IPV victimization, violent offending, violent victimization, and other deviant behaviors. In particular, the gender composition of peer networks may moderate the relationship between gender, IPV victimization, and the deviant behaviors associated with IPV victimization. Peer networks composed mostly of males tend to have a higher level of delinquency (Haynie 2001). This finding is logical considering that males are much more likely than females to engage in offending behaviors. Research has already shown that the gender composition of peer networks can influence violent offending (Haynie, Steffensmeier, and Bell 2007). Haynie and colleagues found that exposure to mostly opposite-sex friendship networks increased violence among females but decreased violence among males. The present research examines whether the gender composition of peer networks also influences the risk of IPV victimization and the behaviors associated with this type of victimization.

For females, having more opposite sex friends could increase the likelihood of IPV victimization, and increase the association between IPV victimization and deviant behaviors, because male-dominated peer networks tend to be less nurturing and more deviant. Compared to female-dominated peer groups, male-dominated peer groups are likely to be more approving of IPV or to hold values that are conducive to abuse against women (DeKeseredy and Schwartz 1997). For males, having more opposite sex friends could decrease the likelihood of IPV victimization and could decrease the association between IPV victimization and deviant behaviors because female-dominated peer networks are more emotionally supportive and conforming. In sum, male-dominated peer groups could exacerbate the relationship between IPV victimization and general and violent offending, while females' peer groups could decrease this same relationship.

SUMMARY

Our current understanding of adolescent IPV is limited compared to our knowledge of adult domestic violence. Also, much of the research on the causes and correlates of partner abuse (for both adolescents and adults) may be superficial and biased due to the limitations in this body of research. This study furthers our understanding of adolescent IPV by examining the relationship between violent offending, violent victimization, and IPV victimization over time. General violence and IPV are usually treated as unique research topics. Some scholars have examined whether IPV is predictive of general violence and criminal offending, but no researchers have considered whether past violent behavior is also predictive of IPV victimization. In other words, the overlap between general violent offending and violent victimization may also extend to this type of victimization (IPV). Evidence that these three phenomena overlap significantly would reveal that general violence and IPV are not as distinct phenomena as some scholars argue. Most research on IPV assumes only one type of IPV: intimate terrorism. That is, most scholars examine the causes and correlates of IPV with the assumption that there is one victim and one offender in each abusive couple. However, evidence from prior research clearly suggests that there are multiple types of IPV, and these multiple types of IPV may have different risk factors and correlates. Some types of IPV may overlap significantly with violent offending and violent victimization (situational couple violence, or mutual aggression), while other types of IPV victimization may overlap only with violent victimization (i.e., intimate terrorism, or one-sided couple violence). This research represents the first systematic study of the causes and correlates of adolescent IPV to distinguish between mutual and one-sided couple abuse.

This is also the first study of adolescent IPV to examine the role of peer network characteristics both in predicting the likelihood of IPV victimization and in examining the correlates of IPV victimization. Criminological research has shown that peer networks play a significant role in delinquency and victimization. Thus, it is important to consider the role of peer networks in this area of research.

The present research first examines adolescent IPV following a framework that is consistent with general violence. The first part of this monograph examines the risk factors for and the consequences of adolescent IPV using a general sample of adolescents involved in romantic partnerships. Consistent with the analyses conducted by Shaffer and Ruback (2002), this study examines the extent to which prior violent offending and violent victimization and IPV victimization overlap. In multivariate analyses, the role of prior violence in predicting subsequent IPV victimization is examined. Then, this study examines the extent to which IPV victimization is predictive of deviant behaviors, including violent offending, violent victimization, delinquency, and drug use. Earlier instances of these behaviors are also controlled for statistically in order to examine whether the relationship between IPV victimization and deviance is spurious.

The next step in the analyses is to distinguish between different types of IPV. Although the Add Health data do not allow for a complete replication of Johnson's (2008) typology of IPV, the present research approximates that framework. The purpose of distinguishing between types of partner violence is to determine whether certain forms of IPV represent a unique class of violent victimization that differs in origins and consequences. In other words, are the risk factors different for different types of IPV, and do the consequences for different types of IPV vary?

For example, we might expect that adolescents who engage in early deviant behaviors (e.g., violent offending, drug use) would be at an increased risk to enter into troublesome relationships, in which the adolescent and his or her partner sometimes engage in violence against one another (situational couple violence, or mutual aggression). Conversely, prior offending and delinquency probably do not explain victimization by intimate terrorism. As for the consequences of IPV, adolescents who are being controlled by their partners through violence are probably less likely to engage in delinquency, but they might be more likely to engage in self-destructive behaviors, such as drug and alcohol use. However, it should be noted that some research has found that females who engage in serious offending are often encouraged to do so by abusive partners (Bowker, Chesney-Lind, and Pollock 1978), and some females engage in violence in response to abusive partners (Ogle, Maier-Katkin, and Bernard 1995).

The analyses reported here also examine the role of gender and friendship networks in these relationships. Is the relationship between general violence, delinquency, drug use, and IPV over time the same or different for male and female adolescents? Also, do the delinquency and gender composition of friendship networks mediate or moderate these relationships? These questions will be explored in Chapters 4 and 5.

CHAPTER 2

An Integrated Theoretical Approach to General Violence and Intimate Partner Violence among Adolescents

INTRODUCTION

The purpose of this research is to understand the relationships between general violence, delinquency, drug use, and IPV victimization over time. Several theories of criminal behavior and victimization are relevant to this study, including opportunity theories (routine activities and lifestyle exposure), strain theory, and differential association and social learning theories. Some of these theories are more useful for understanding the risk factors for IPV victimization (e.g., opportunity theories), while others are better for explaining the adverse consequences that are associated with IPV victimization (e.g., strain theory). In this chapter, the theoretical implications of these theories for this study are described.

OPPORTUNITY THEORIES

One of the most important types of theories for explaining the relationship between general violence and IPV victimization relates to opportunity. This category includes routine activities theory (Cohen and Felson 1979) and, especially, lifestyle exposure theory (Hindelang et al. 1978; for a review of both theories, see Meier and Miethe 1993).

Both theories posit that crime rates and rates of victimization vary with general patterns of routine activities (Meier and Miethe 1993). The main differences between these two theories are in terminology and the original purpose of each theory. Routine activities theory was initially developed to explain changes in crime rates over time and space at the aggregate level, and lifestyle exposure theory was developed by Hindelang and colleagues specifically to explain the risk of victimization.

The development of routine activities theory presented a noteworthy shift in criminological theory. Unlike other theories, this theory focused on how situations can be motivating rather than focusing on offender motivations. That is, situations provide or prevent opportunities for crime. Routine activities theory describes three necessary conditions for a crime to occur: a motivated offender, a suitable target, and the absence of a capable guardian (Cohen and Felson 1979). Cohen and Felson explained aggregate changes in crime rates by looking at societal changes, including the increasing presence of the automobile and mass transportation and the movement of people, particularly females, out of the household. For example, the automobile has dispersed peoples' activities away from the home, making the cars and the people suitable targets in situations with few capable guardians. Also, as people spend more and more time outside of their homes (particularly women who have increasingly entered the work force), their homes became more accessible to burglars.

Felson (1998) further described how changes in society influenced criminal opportunity. For example, advanced technology has made durable goods smaller and easier to steal. Also, young people are more mobile now, and have more access to areas where there are few parents or adults present. The point of routine activities is not to understand why individuals commit crime, or in this case employ violence, but rather how lifestyles, situations, and opportunities influence the likelihood of crime occurrence.

Several empirical studies have investigated the relationship between routine activities and criminal victimization. Miethe, Stafford, and Long (1987) used a routine activities approach to examine demographic differences in criminal victimization. The authors theorized that individuals who spend more time outside of the home, especially at night, are at greater risk for criminal victimization. Time spent outside of the home is considered a function of risk because individuals are more physically proximate to others, especially strangers, and activity outside of the home is usually more patterned and predictable. Miethe et al. (1987) found empirical evidence to support their propositions. However, time spent outside of the home is a better predictor of property victimization than violent victimization. Miethe and his associates speculate that routine activities theory is less useful for understanding violent crime than property crime because this type of crime is more personal, spontaneous, and irrational (Miethe et al. 1987).

Time spent outside of the home can at least partially explain violent victimizations that are perpetrated by strangers. Thus, this conceptualization of opportunity theory can explain non-partner-related violent victimizations, but not IPV victimization. Intimate partner violence requires interpersonal confrontation by individuals known by one another. It is less about exploiting opportunity, and more about using aggression to achieve various goals (e.g., control, compliance).

Unlike routine activities theory, lifestyle exposure theory is better able to explain both general violent victimization and IPV victimization. Lifestyle exposure theory explains the relationship between demographic characteristics, personal habits, and the risk of victimization (Hindelang et al., 1978). Criminologists have consistently found that males, unmarried individuals, young people, and people from economically disadvantaged groups have the highest rates of victimization. According to lifestyle exposure theory, this relationship is likely mediated by the lifestyles and activities of these demographic groups (Lauritsen et al.1991).

Young, single men from a lower class background are more likely to "hang out" in public places, such as bars, pool halls, and local malls (Hindelang et al. 1978). These are also the demographic characteristics most associated with delinquency and offending. Thus, young, single, and disadvantaged men are the most likely to be in settings conducive to victimization, to engage in delinquency, and to spend more time with individuals who share these demographic and lifestyle characteristics (Lauritsen et al. 1991). Several studies have demonstrated these relationships (e.g., Miethe et al., 1987; Wittebrood and Niewbeerta, 2000). Other studies have found that women socialize less outside of the home and have lower rates of victimization (Forde and Kennedy, 1997).

Sampson and Lauritsen (1994) found that young males who reported both violent behavior and minor deviance had a higher risk of victimization. This relationship between offending and victimization makes sense insofar as offenders are more likely to have ready cash or goods from their crimes and they are less likely to report their victimizations to police. Researchers consistently find that offenders and victims have similar characteristics and engage in similar behaviors (Gottfredson 1981; Hindelang 1976; Lauritsen et al. 1991; Menard 2002; for a review see Schreck et al. 2008).

Offending and victimization are highly correlated and share many of the same risk factors, especially age. Adolescents have the highest rates of both offending and victimization (Lauritsen et al. 1991; Lauritsen and Quinet 1995). Both of these phenomena are likely explained by opportunity. The high rate of victimization among adolescents is likely explained by their proximity and exposure to criminal behavior, their attractiveness as targets (e.g., their inability to defend themselves, the valuable goods they carry), and their frequent lack of guardianship (Miethe and Meier 1994). In addition to placing offenders in close proximity with other offenders and away from authority figures, adolescent offending may also provoke attack by other offenders (Jensen and Brownfield 1986). Also, adolescent offenders make attractive targets for victimization because their outlaw status makes them less likely to report their victimization to authorities.

Adolescents probably have a higher rate of offending because they have more opportunities to engage in deviance. Osgood et al. (1996) found that unstructured time spent in the presence of peers and in the absence of supervising adults was correlated with delinquency. The authors explained that the absence of adults provides opportunity and the presence of peers provides encouragement to engage in delinquency. Given that delinquency is commonly a group activity, delinquency places adolescents in close proximity to other offenders. The absence of adult supervision places adolescent offenders away from guardianship. Osgood and his colleagues concluded that motivations reside in situations. In other words, things that teenagers might do in a park or a home without adults – smoke, drink, graffiti – they would not do in a classroom or church.

Lifestyle exposure theory is typically used to explain property and violent victimizations, rather than IPV victimization, probably because IPV is generally studied and understood apart from general victimization. This separation is likely due to the fact that these two forms of violence (general violence and IPV) are gendered. That is, one type of violence (general violence) is dominated by males (both as victims and offenders), and is the focus of general criminological studies. Intimate partner violence, on the other hand, has many more female victims and has been adopted as a feminist issue.

Violence researchers, such as Hindelang et al. (1978), who used lifestyle exposure theory to explain the overlap between violent offending and violent victimization, probably did not consider (or at least did not write) that the victim-offender overlap that applies to general violence might also apply to partner violence. Intimate partner violence researchers, such as Straus and Gelles (1986, 1990), have found an overlap between IPV victims and abusers (i.e., situational couple violence), but they did not describe whether this overlap extends to general violence. Intimate partner violence victimization has been linked with other deviant behaviors (including violence and delinquency), but these behaviors are considered to be *outcomes* of IPV victimization. However, it is conceivable that violent experiences during adolescence (both as victims and offenders) affect the risk of IPV victimization. In sum, there are two related, yet separate, lines of research that do not appear to be aware of one-another: (1) the victim-offender overlap in general violence; and, (2) the victim-offender overlap in IPV (situational couple violence).This study integrates these two lines of research.

The overlap between violent offending, violent victimization, and IPV victimization can be explained by lifestyle exposure theory. According to this theory, an individual's risk of victimization is proportional to his or her exposure to high-risk situations and offenders (Meier and Miethe 1993). Adolescents who engage in violent offending are exposed to high risk situations that leave them vulnerable to both partner and non-partner related victimizations. The purpose of the present study is not to place blame on victims of IPV, but rather to demonstrate how early violent behaviors place youth at risk for IPV victimization. This research examines the relationship between general violence, adolescent delinquency, drug use, and IPV victimization over time.

Based on the propositions from routine activities and lifestyle exposure theories, non-relationship violent victimization and violent offending can be related to subsequent IPV victimization for three reasons. First, adolescents who engage in delinquency are likely to associate with other delinquents (Akers et al. 1979; Haynie 2002), and they probably select their intimate partners from these friendship groups. Selecting an intimate partner from a network of delinquent peers increases the likelihood of partner abuse because individuals who engage in delinquency and crime are also more likely to perpetrate partner abuse (Connolly et al. 2000; Moffitt et al. 2006). Thus, adolescent offenders are more likely to become romantically involved with an offender. Consistent with this expectation, Simons et al. (1993) found that adolescent women who were abused as young children were inclined to engage in deviant behavior and to become involved in abusive relationships. The relationship between early parental maltreatment and later delinquency and IPV victimization was attributed to assortative mating and partner selection from delinquent peer groups. Abusive romantic relationships are likely embedded in a larger network of delinquent peers.

Second, the propensity to engage in offending and other aggressive behaviors may cause conflict within a romantic relationship, and this conflict could be conducive to couple violence. This scenario is most likely to occur among victims and perpetrators of situational couple violence (or mutual partner violence). In other words, if both partners in a couple engage in delinquency and other aggressive acts it is they are probably more likely to have a tumultuous and conflict-ridden partnership than non-offenders because they are probably more likely to act aggressively towards their partners and more likely to provoke their partners into violence.

The last way that the victim-offender overlap may apply to teen dating violence is that adolescents who already engage in criminal behavior might make attractive targets for dating violence, given that they are less inclined to report victimizations to the authorities. Just as offenders make rather attractive targets for both property and violent crime in general (Hindelang et al. 1978), they may also make attractive targets for partner abuse.

Following the logic of routine activities and lifestyle exposure theories, peer networks might influence violent behaviors and IPV victimization in two specific ways. First, having a large network of delinquent peers should have a positive association with both offending and partner abuse. Delinquent peers encourage deviant behaviors; having delinquent peers increases self-reported delinquency (e.g., Haynie 2001; Warr and Stafford 1991). Also, if the adolescent enters an abusive relationship, deviant peers may be less likely to intervene and report abuse to parents or authorities. Conforming, pro-social peers could be thought of as "capable guardians," and the absence of non-delinquent peers likely increases the risk of IPV victimization (Cohen and Felson 1979). Being embedded in a large network of delinquent friends should have a positive association with intimate partner abuse and offending.

Second, routine activities and lifestyle exposure theories would predict that having no peers will be negatively correlated with general offending and positively correlated with victimization by a partner. This expectation follows from research by Demuth (2004) and Kreager (2004) who found that adolescents isolated from peer networks are less likely to offend. Also, given that these "loners" do not have much contact with their contemporaries, they might be less likely to enter a romantic partnership. However, if they do engage in a romantic relationship, they would make ideal targets for abuse, given that they do not have friends to prevent or stop partner abuse.

Based on the theories and prior research described above, this study should reveal a relationship between Wave One violent behavior, delinquent peer associations, and unstructured socializing (Osgood et al. 1996) and Wave Two IPV victimization. Attachment to delinquent peer networks, as with violent offending, represents exposure to a risk of victimization. Also, given that individuals tend to select romantic partners from peer networks, adolescents embedded in deviant peer networks likely select deviant partners. As described before, deviant partners are more likely to be abusive partners.

Unstructured socializing creates situations conducive to victimization. The absence of parents, authority figures, and other responsible adults leaves adolescents more vulnerable to victimization.

If present, responsible adults could prevent adolescents from engaging in delinquency and violence, and they could intervene in abusive relationships.

Also based on previous research, general violence (both offending and victimization) and delinquent behavior should be related over time (Menard 2002; Shaffer and Ruback 2002). Prior violence and delinquency are predictive of subsequent victimization and deviant behaviors, including IPV victimization, general violence, delinquency, and drug use. Additionally, this model anticipates that Wave Two IPV victimization is also related to Wave Two general violence, delinquency and drug use.

GENERAL STRAIN THEORY

Given that strain theories explain the relationship between adverse situations and offending behavior, this type of theory has obvious implications for the present study. Strain theory has several forms in the criminology literature. The basic premise behind all strain theories is that some individuals are not "treated as [they] want to be treated" (Agnew 1992, 48), and this strain may lead some to engage in deviant behavior.

Classic strain theories, such as the ones developed by Merton (1938), Cohen (1955), and Cloward and Ohlin (1960), placed an emphasis on strain caused by an inability to achieve material wealth. Merton (1938) argued that differences in crime rates across societies were tied to the extent to which cultures emphasized monetary success and allowed open access to that success. According to Merton's theory, a disjuncture between the emphasis on material wealth and legitimate access to that wealth (e.g., education, hard work) create a state of "anomie" (normlessness), which could lead to crime in a variety of ways. Classic strain theories have a macro perspective focused primarily on monetary success as the source of strain. Thus, these strain theories are not useful for understanding a specific individual-level phenomenon such as the relationships between abusive romantic partnerships and offending behavior.

Agnew's (1992) general strain theory (GST), the version that is applicable to this study, has a much broader definition of strain and is more relevant to individual-level behavior. Agnew's GST is focused on personal relationships and adverse situations and how these factors can influence deviant behavior. Rather than focusing on one major source of strain, as in Merton's conception (i.e., the need for wealth and inability to legitimately attain it), GST includes three major sources of strain, each of which may be actual or anticipated: (1) blocked access to desired goals; (2) removal of positively valued stimuli; and, (3) exposure to harmful stimuli. The experience of strain places individuals in a negative affective state (e.g., sadness, frustration, anger), which forces them to take corrective actions. Agnew placed a heavy emphasis on how certain emotions, especially anger, can lead to crime. Although anger is most associated with crime, other emotions, including guilt, fear, anxiety, and depression may also lead to criminal behavior. Individuals may choose to respond or adapt to strain in a variety of ways, ranging from healthy law-abiding behavior to criminal behavior. The ways in which individuals adapt to strain depends on several factors, including past experiences with strain, the environment in which they were raised, and temperament. For example, prior experiences with violent offending and violent victimization could leave some adolescents predisposed to react to strain with adverse corrective actions (e.g., violent behavior or drug use).

Agnew's GST has obvious implications for this study. In particular, GST could explain why adolescents react to IPV victimization with violent offending, delinquency, and/or drug use. The third type of strain that Agnew described, the actual or anticipated exposure to harmful stimuli, is directly applicable to the focus of the present study, IPV victimization. Adverse corrective actions may result from IPV victimization when individuals try either to avoid or minimize abuse, or victims may seek revenge against their abusers (Agnew 1992). This study posits that strain, in the form of IPV victimization, may cause adolescents to feel anger, frustration, or depression feelings, which can lead to corrective action. The action taken could be destructive behaviors (e.g., violent offending, delinquency) or it could be self-destructive behaviors (e.g., drug use).

An individual's prior experiences with violence (both offending and victimization) may be indicative of how an individual will react to this type of strain. Also, as described in the section on opportunity theories, prior antisocial behavior may be a risk factor for experiencing intimate partner abuse. Other factors, including parental attachment or supportive friendship networks, for example, may condition the relationship between strain and negative affective states. Adolescents who have close, positive relationships with their parents probably experience less strain and are less likely to engage in deviant behaviors. And when these closely attached adolescents do experience strain, they are probably less likely to resort to deviant behaviors because they have the guidance and support of their parents. Also, adolescents who are attached to conforming peer groups have supportive friends who can help them through difficult situations (i.e., strain) and dissuade them from adverse corrective actions (e.g., delinquency, drug use).

Related to the present study, strain caused by IPV victimization should be more manageable if the victim has positive non-delinquent friendship network. Conforming friendship networks work as protective factors, leaving victims of IPV less likely to engage in violence, delinquency, or drug abuse. Conversely, adolescents who are connected to deviant peer groups are more likely to experience strain and to resort to deviant forms of corrective actions. Negative relationships with parents and friendships with deviant others can both create strain and exacerbate the negative feelings associated with strain.

IPV victimization is the primary source of strain in this study. Prior violent behavior affects both whether the respondent becomes the victim of IPV and the affective state that comes as a result of strain. Peer networks may interact with strain by either influencing the negative affective state into which the adolescent enters as a result of strain or by influencing the corrective action taken by the adolescent. For example, adolescents who have fewer delinquent peer networks may be less likely to experience anger or depression as a result of strain. Or, by having these positive influences in their lives, these adolescents may be better equipped to deal with feelings of anger and depression in a healthy and constructive manner.

Males and females may have qualitatively distinct experiences with strain, which lead to differences in how the sexes react to external stressors (Broidy and Agnew 1997; Piquero and Sealock 2004). Both genders experience similar amounts of strain (e.g., financial stress, family conflict); however, males and females are more vulnerable to different types of strain because males and females tend to hold different values. Males, more than females, are focused on economic goals, making them more sensitive to financial strain. Broidy and Agnew (1997) theorized that financial strain is more likely to lead to property crime and violence, a pattern that would explain the over-representation of males in these two types of crimes. However, with the rise of female-headed households, females have become increasingly vulnerable to financial strain. This phenomenon could explain increases in rates of female property and violent crime.

Compared to males, females are more likely to experience strain related to personal relationships, social control, and the burden of taking care of others (Broidy and Agnew 1997). These sources of strain usually inhibit most deviant behaviors, although they may lead to depressive symptoms that are more conducive to self-destructive behaviors (e.g., drug use).

Males and females also vary in their emotional reactions to strain. Both genders experience similar levels of anger in response to strain, however for females feelings of anger are often coupled with other emotions such as guilt or depression. Gender roles and expectations make it less acceptable for women to express anger. Further, males tend to be more confident, possess higher self-esteem on average, and generally feel more empowered to deal with strain in an aggressive manner (Broidy and Agnew 1997). Feeling less empowered and confident, females are more likely to resort to self-destructive behaviors to deal with strain.

Because males and females have different types of friendship networks, the relationship between strain, negative affective states, and corrective actions are likely to be different as well (Broidy and Agnew 1997). Females generally have smaller, more intimate friendship circles than males. Given that females are on average more law-abiding than males, female friendship networks are probably also less delinquent than male friendship networks. Therefore, taken together, these two facts mean that female friendship networks are likely to act as protective factors for females in response to strain.

Male friendship networks are different. In addition to being larger, less intimate, and more delinquent, they are also more competitive and less nurturing. Thus, male friendship networks should exacerbate the effects of strain for male victims and increase negative outcomes. Consistent with this proposition, Haynie et al. (2007) found that opposite-sex friendship networks influence male and female violent offending in different ways. For females, having more male friends is associated with an increase in violent offending. For males, having more female friends is associated with a decrease in violent offending.

In the present study, two outcomes are expected based on Agnew's (1992) GST and Broidy and Agnew's (1997) interpretation of GST. First, IPV, as an indicator of strain, should be positively associated with delinquency, violence, and drug use. This link between strain and deviant behaviors should be at least partially mediated by negative feelings, such as depression. Not only should prior antisocial behavior increase the likelihood that individuals experience intimate partner abuse (i.e., strain), but it should also increase the likelihood that the corrective actions that they take are criminal.

Second, gender should moderate the relationship between IPV victimization and deviant behaviors. In other words, the negative affective states (i.e., the emotions) between abuse and antisocial behaviors, the types of antisocial behaviors associated with intimate partner abuse, and the protective factors that influence the relationship between IPV victimization and deviant behaviors should be different for males and females. Following Broidy and Agnew's (1997) theoretical arguments, female respondents should be more negatively influenced by strain induced by IPV, and they should be more likely to engage in drug use, as opposed to general delinquency and violent offending. Consistent with this expectation, research has shown that female victims of IPV experience more long-lasting mental health and drug use problems as compared to male victims (Ackard et al. 2007; Olshen et al. 2007). Further, in a test of Broidy and Agnew's propositions about gender and GST, Mazerolle (1998) found that reactions to strain did vary between males and females. Males were more likely to externalize their anger as a result of strain and engage in violent behavior. Females, on the other hand, engaged in more self-destructive behaviors as a result of strain.

The gender composition of friendship networks should influence the type of deviant behavior that results from IPV victimization. Having more female friends should decrease the likelihood of violent offending and delinquency for all respondents, and having more male friends should increase the likelihood of these same outcomes.

For male victims of IPV, Agnew's (1992) GST would predict that the link between IPV victimization and deviant behavior is mediated more by anger or frustration than depression. Also, males are more likely to externalize their strain-induced anger in the form of violent offending or delinquency, as opposed to drug use. Given the large, impersonal, criminogenic nature of male friendship networks, same-sex friendship networks should positively interact with strain and anger in their effects on illicit and self-destructive behaviors for male victims.

DIFFERENTIAL ASSOCIATION AND SOCIAL LEARNING THEORIES

Differential association theory, originally introduced by Sutherland and colleagues in 1934, assumes that criminal behavior is learned like any other behavior (Sutherland, Cressey, and Luckenbill 1992). Cultures contain various "definitions," or messages, that are either favorable or unfavorable to violation of the law and established norms. These messages are transmitted through various outlets, including friends, family, and teachers.

Whether an individual adopts more messages favorable to deviance than conformity depends on variables such as how early he or she was exposed to the deviant messages, the length and frequency of the exposure, and the importance of the person or group that is delivering the messages. Individuals are more likely to adopt definitions from personal and intimate contacts. In addition to adopting definitions, individuals must also learn deviant or conforming behaviors, including techniques, motives, rationalizations, and attitudes.

Thus, an individual surrounded by positive and conforming role models in a healthy environment would learn messages favorable to following laws and norms. Not only would the individual have to learn how to conform (e.g., attend school, listen to teachers, follow school rules), he or she would also have to learn the value of conforming (e.g., graduating from school, achieving gainful employment, independence). An individual surrounded by delinquent peers in a criminogenic neighborhood would likely adopt more definitions favorable to violation of the law. Crime results from an excess of learned messages favorable to law violation. Thus, once an individual adopts more messages favorable to deviance rather than conformity, the individual adopts techniques of criminal behavior and values such behavior.

Burgess and Akers (1966; Akers 1985) modified Sutherland's original theory by adding learning mechanisms developed by Skinner (1953). According to Akers (1985), Sutherland focused on definitions and the avenues in which these definitions are transmitted, but not on how individuals successfully adopt these definitions. The resulting social learning theory (or differential association-reinforcement theory) was composed of Sutherland's original principles coupled with elements of social learning and positive and negative reinforcement developed by psychologists. To adopt definitions favorable to the violation of the law successfully, individuals must perceive greater rewards from criminal and deviant behavior than from conforming behavior. Delinquent peers provide an ideal setting for learning and adopting a deviant lifestyle, given that delinquent peers can teach adolescents how to engage in illegal behaviors and can reward and encourage these behaviors. Adolescents from disadvantaged backgrounds are also more likely to adopt a deviant lifestyle because they are frequently residing in criminogenic neighborhoods that lack positive role models.

According to social learning theory, people are more likely to engage in criminal and deviant behavior when four conditions are met: (1) they are exposed to others who support and engage in criminal behavior; (2) the negative behavior is reinforced by others; (3) they are exposed to more criminal or deviant behavior than conforming behavior; and, (4) they have adopted more definitions favorable to violation of the law and established norms (Akers 1985, 51).

One of the main propositions of differential association and social learning theories is that deviance and the process of learning deviance is a group phenomenon. Consistent with this proposition, research has consistently shown that individuals who have criminal or deviant peer associations are more likely to engage in deviance (e.g., Haynie 2001, 2002; Warr and Stafford 1991). Interactions with friends are central to the lives of adolescents, and there is a consensus among criminologists that peers exert a strong influence on criminal behavior (e.g., Giordano et al. 1986). Indeed, two of the most consistent findings in the criminology literature are as follows: (1) delinquency occurs in a group setting; and, (2) the delinquency of peers is the strongest predictor of self-reported delinquency (Haynie 2002). For example, Haynie (2002) found that most adolescents are involved in friendship networks composed of both deviant and non-deviant peers, and having friendship networks with larger proportions of deviant peers is predictive of an individual's subsequent delinquent behavior.

If delinquent peer networks influence an individual's deviant behavior, then it is reasonable to expect that intimate partners have a similar influence. Indeed, Haynie el al. (2005) found that an intimate partner's delinquency affects an individual's deviant behavior above and beyond the effect of peer network delinquency. As stated previously, many perpetrators of IPV also engage in other delinquency and offending behaviors (Connolly et al. 2000; Moffitt et al. 2006). Moffitt et al. (2006) found that there is considerable overlap between intimate partner abuse and other criminal behavior. Although different constructs and personality types explain the perpetration of partner abuse and engaging in other types of criminal behavior, intimate partner abusers also commonly engage in other types of criminal behavior. Therefore, perpetrators of intimate partner abuse likely have a negative orientation to following the law, exposing an individual to messages favorable to deviance.

Mulford and Giordano (2008) argued that peers have a large influence on romantic relationships during adolescence. Peers are more important to individuals during adolescence than during adulthood, and friends play a large role in romantic relationships during adolescence (Adelman and Kil 2007). For example, Molidor and Tolman (1998) interviewed middle and high school students and found that about half of all adolescent couples' violence occurred in the presence of others. Moreover, boys reported that they would be more likely to engage in couple violence if provoked in front of their peers.

Based on differential association and social learning theories, delinquent peer networks and involvement in an abusive romantic relationship provide ideal settings for the acquisition of deviant lifestyles for adolescents. These theories might also explain how adolescents enter into abusive relationships. Adolescents who engage in delinquency early on have more delinquent contacts and more favorable associations with deviance. These adolescents could be more susceptible or receptive to deviant romantic partners who engage in abusive behavior. These propositions were demonstrated in Miller's (2001) study of male and female gang members. Miller found that early deviant behavior and abusive home environments were the primary factors predicting gang membership. Once in gangs, females were more likely to enter into abusive relationships.

The ways in which GST and differential association and social learning theories explain the relationship between IPV victimization and deviant behavior are not radically different. However, the mechanisms are different. As described earlier, negative emotional states should be highly predictive of deviant behavior according to GST. With differential association and social learning theories, on the other hand, anger, anxiety and depression have little to do with whether an individual enters a deviant lifestyle. Rather, differential association and social learning theories predict deviance when an individual has deviant contacts, learns and adopts the lifestyle, and finds it more rewarding than a conforming lifestyle.

SUMMARY OF THE THEORETICAL FRAMEWORK AND INTEGRATED MODEL

All of the theories described above predict a link between IPV victimization and deviant behavior. Both opportunity theories and social learning theories are able to explain how deviant behavior is both a risk-factor and an outcome of IPV victimization, while Agnew's GST is better able to explain why deviant behavior results from IPV victimization. Peers exert a significant influence based on all three theories.

The main differences between these theories are the mediators and moderators that link early offending, victimization, and subsequent offending. Routine activities and lifestyle exposure theories predict that exposure to risk mediates the relationship between offending and victimization. Exposure to risk is a nebulous concept and is sometimes difficult to measure. The present study captures exposure to risk by measuring the delinquency of the friendship networks to which the respondents are connected and the amount of time they spend in unstructured activities. Given that several studies have already linked deviant peer networks and unstructured socializing to individual deviance, it is reasonable to expect that peer networks will exert an influence on deviant behavior and IPV victimization.

Based on Agnew's GST, the effect of IPV victimization on deviant behavior should be at least partially mediated by emotional states such as depression. Ideally, multiple psychological factors should be included in the models for a true test of Agnew's GST. However, the Add Health data do not include all of the relevant psychological factors. The only psychological measure included in Add Health is depression, and it is included in all of the models presented in this monograph. Moreover, the analyses examine whether it works as a mediator between IPV victimization and deviant behavior, especially for female victims and drug use.

Also, unlike the other two theories described, the type of illicit behavior that is affected and the strength of the relationship should vary. Agnew's GST and Broidy and Agnew's (1997) gendered interpretation of GST would be supported if the deviant behaviors associated with strain (IPV victimization) varied across male and female victims. Females should be more likely to engage in drug use as a result of IPV victimization, and less likely to engage in violent offending and general delinquency as compared to male respondents.

All three theories predict that delinquent peer networks increase offending, but Broidy and Agnew (1997) focus more specifically on same-sex friendship networks. These authors would predict that same-sex friendship networks moderate the relationship between IPV victimization and deviant behavior. This interaction should decrease the likelihood of violent offending and delinquency for females victims of IPV, and have the opposite effect for male victims. The intimate and supportive nature of female friendship networks should decrease the likelihood of offending and substance use for females, while the competitive, emotionally distant, and delinquent nature of male friendship networks should increase offending and substance use for male adolescents.

Evidence of peer influence on deviant behavior and IPV victimization would support the propositions of differential association and social learning theories. These propositions are not unique to differential association and social learning theories; these are also factors based on opportunity theories and Agnew's GST. However, it is not possible to directly measure whether respondents in the Add Health data have adopted pro-deviant attitudes. In the questionnaire there are no questions that specifically address the adolescents' attitudes towards rules and laws (e.g., whether they believe the rules are worth following, whether they hold values in opposition to community norms and legal codes).

This study combines aspects of lifestyle exposure theory, strain theory, and differential association theory to explain the likelihood of IPV victimization and the effects of this type of victimization on behavior. Early delinquency, violent offending, violent victimization, drug use, and delinquent peer associations should all be correlated, and they should all exert a direct effect on IPV victimization. Prior violent offending, and violent victimization should influence IPV victimization through depression, especially for female victims. Given that the best predictor of future behavior is past behavior, early instances of violent offending, delinquency, and drug use should be the strongest predictors of wave two occurrences of these behaviors. However, IPV victimization should still have a direct effect on these deviant behaviors, net of early behaviors.

MUTUAL AND ONE-SIDED IPV VICTIMIZATION

The above theoretical framework is intended to apply to all IPV victimizations, although it is probably more applicable to what Johnson (2008) called situational couple violence. For the purposes of the present study, it is assumed to be most applicable to mutual IPV victimization (i.e., in the secure romantic data, when both linked partners report IPV victimization). Some of the theories described above are more useful for explaining mutual IPV victimization, while others are more capable of explaining one-sided IPV victimization.

Lifestyle exposure theory is better able to explain mutual IPV victimization than one-sided IPV victimization. According to this theory, mutual IPV victimization can be explained as exposure to risk through offending behaviors and delinquent peer associations. Adolescents who engage in violence likely have more deviant peer associations. Moreover, these deviant peer networks and their own violent behavior leave them more vulnerable to general violent victimization and IPV victimization, given that they likely pick their partners from the peer networks in which they are embedded. Individuals who display early violent behaviors are probably more likely to be violent in their relationships, and because they pick their romantic partners from the same peer networks, their partners probably have the same disposition. Thus, adolescents who engage in prior violent behaviors are probably more likely to end up in mutually aggressive relationships.

Unlike victims of mutual IPV, this study does not expect that victims of one-sided IPV will have engaged in prior violent behaviors or have had more deviant peer associations. Rather, victims of one-sided IPV are likely to have been victimized earlier, either by parental maltreatment or general non-partner-related victimization.

For one-sided IPV victimization, an explanation for repeat victimization (often referred to as state dependence and population heterogeneity; Lauritsen and Quinet 1995) is likely to be useful. That is, prior victimization somehow alters an individual (e.g., behavior, psychological well-being), which in turn increases the risk of future victimization. For one-sided IPV victimization, prior general violent victimization may alter the victim's psychological well-being or behavior (e.g., Cougle, Resnick, and Kilpatrick 2009; Norris and Kaniasty 1991), which in turn affects the likelihood that the individual will enter into an abusive relationship. Additionally, some individuals may have a general predisposition to become victims (Hodges and Perry 1999; Lauritsen and Quinet 1999; Wittebrood and Nieuwbeerta 2000).

Strain theory is useful for explaining the consequences of both mutual and one-sided IPV victimization, although the reactions to strain should vary based on the type of IPV victimization. Mutual couple aggression is probably more strongly associated with subsequent violent offending and delinquency, given the existing violent propensities of individuals involved in mutual couple aggression. That is, individuals who are already violent are probably more likely to engage in mutual couple violence, and this couple violence could motivate subsequent violent offending and delinquency.

One-sided IPV victimization is probably also associated with violent offending and delinquency, but the association with drug use is likely stronger. Victims of one-sided IPV are usually female, and females tend to react to strain with more self-destructive behaviors such as drug use. Because female victims of abuse often engage in other deviant behaviors (Chesney-Lind 1997), this research expects to find that one-sided IPV will also be associated with general delinquency and, possibly, violent offending.

In sum, this study expects that prior violent offending is predictive of mutual IPV victimization, while prior violent victimization is predictive of one-sided IPV victimization. Mutual IPV victimization is associated with short-term (i.e., same-wave) violent offending and delinquency, while one-sided IPV victimization is associated with short-time general violent victimization (non-partner-related) and drug use.

GENERAL HYPOTHESES

1. Early (Wave One) violent victimization and violent offending will influence the likelihood of Wave Two IPV victimization. This hypothesis is based on the premise that early violent offending and violent victimization leave adolescents more vulnerable to entering into abusive relationships. As described by opportunity theories, individuals who engage in criminal behaviors make more attractive victims and they are more likely to engage in behaviors that provoke victimization. Also, engaging in criminal and delinquent behavior leaves deviant adolescents more exposed to deviant others, and more exposure can increase the risk of victimization. This exposure also increases the likelihood that an individual will select a deviant romantic partner because he or she is more likely to select a mate from the people he or she is around the most. Finally, based on the general violence literature, there is consistency in victimization over time. That is, prior victimization is highly predictive of subsequent victimization. A small proportion of victims usually account for a disproportionate amount of victimizations.

2. IPV victimization will positively increase the likelihood of violent offending, general violent victimization (non-partner related), general delinquency, and drug use, controlling for prior instances of these same behaviors. This hypothesis is consistent with research that has linked IPV victimization with a variety of antisocial behaviors, as well as

research that has linked non-relationship victimization to offending. Based on the criminological literature, this outcome is a reasonable expectation because deviant behavior and victimization are both highly correlated. Just as offending and victimization predict one another, it is reasonable to expect that this type of victimization (IPV) has a similar relationship with deviant outcomes and subsequent victimization. Several studies have linked IPV victimization to a variety of deviant outcomes, although many of these studies did not control for prior instances of these same behaviors. Prior deviant behaviors are highly predictive of future deviant behaviors, and violent offending, delinquency, and drug use may explain both IPV victimization and these outcomes. In other words, the demonstrated relationship between IPV victimization and deviant outcomes may be spurious. This study proposes that this relationship is not spurious, and will control for prior instances of these behaviors to ensure the validity of this relationship.

3. Peer network characteristics will both influence the likelihood of IPV victimization and the outcomes associated with IPV victimization. Given that prior research has established the strong influence of peers on delinquency, peer networks should influence offending behavior and IPV victimization based on the popularity of the respondent and the delinquency and gender composition of his or her peer group. Individuals with few or no friends are less likely to enter into romantic partnerships. However, if they do enter into relationships, they will not have friends who can identify and report abuse or intervene. Also, most adolescent peer groups have at least low levels of delinquency. Higher levels of delinquency in peer groups will positively influence offending and IPV victimization. Finally, mostly male peer groups should positively influence both offending and IPV victimization, while mostly female peer groups should negatively influence offending and IPV victimization.

4. The relationship between deviant behavior and IPV victimization will vary between male and female victims. Males and females have different experiences with general violence, IPV, and other deviant behaviors. Males and females differ in their pathways to offending, and they are vulnerable to different types of victimizations. When males are victimized by IPV, it is more likely to be the result of mutually

aggressive partnerships than intimate terrorism. Thus, past violent offending should be a stronger predictor of IPV victimization for males than for females. Given the strong relationships between victimization and offending for females, past victimization should be a stronger predictor of IPV victimization for females than for males. In response to IPV victimization, males and females will likely engage in different types of deviant behaviors. Males are probably more likely to engage in subsequent delinquency and violent offending, whereas females are probably more likely to cope with IPV with more self-destructive behaviors such as drug use.

5. Both the risk factors for IPV victimization and the outcomes of IPV victimization should vary depending on whether the partner violence was one-sided or mutual. The risk factors and effects of IPV should be different depending on whether relationship violence is one-sided or mutual. We should not expect a female adolescent who is being terrorized by her partner to engage in delinquency, given the controlling nature of her relationship. Victims of one-sided abuse are likely to be under close surveillance or their behaviors are micro-managed, consistent with intimate terrorism (Johnson 2008) or coercive control (Stark 2007). That is, we should expect victims of one-sided violence to engage in less delinquency and less violent behavior than victims of mutually aggressive relationships. Victims of one-sided abuse are more likely to engage in more self-destructive behaviors, such as drug, tobacco, and alcohol use. The one caveat to this prediction concerns females' involvement in crime because they have been forced to do so. That is, some serious female offending has been motivated by abusive partners (Bowker et al. 1978), and some females engage in violence in response to abusive partners (Ogle et al. 1995).

CHAPTER 3

An Overview of the National Longitudinal Study of Adolescent Health

INTRODUCTION

The data for this project came from the National Longitudinal Study of Adolescent Health (Add Health), which is the largest nationally representative longitudinal study of adolescents ever completed. The study, conducted by the Carolina Population Center at the University of North Carolina at Chapel Hill, began in 1994 and 1995 with a sample of 90,118 adolescents in grades 7 through 12 from schools throughout the United States. To collect this sample, the administrators of this survey used a clustered sampling design based on a stratified sample of 80 high schools and 52 "feeder" middle schools (matched to the selected high schools).

The Add Health data provided this research with three advantages over previous studies of adolescent IPV. First, the longitudinal design of this survey allowed for an examination of the timing of adolescent IPV victimization relative to violent offending, non-partner related violent victimization, and other deviant behaviors. The present study is an examination of offending and victimization (including IPV victimization) over time. Other studies have found that this relationship is reciprocal—that is, offending is predictive of victimization and victimization is predictive of offending (e.g., Lauritsen et al. 1991; Shaffer and Ruback 2002). Thus, it is important to have longitudinal data to examine this complex reciprocal relationship.

The second major advantage of using Add Health data is that, because there was a large sample of adolescents, relatively rare events were included in the data. These data included a large enough sample to capture some female offending, even though females are less likely to engage in delinquency and criminal behavior. Also, there was a large enough sample to capture a substantial number of IPV victims. Additionally, there was a large enough sample to capture an adequate amount of male and female IPV victimization for analysis. Males are less likely to be the victims of serious violent partner abuse, but these data included enough instances of IPV victimization to allow for a comparison between males and females.

The third advantage of using Add Health data was the extensive network data present. Measuring peer delinquency based on responses from the respondent may create inaccurate measures. Respondents tend to overestimate the similarities between themselves and their peers, which can create inflated estimates of peer delinquency. The peer network data in Add Health allowed for a more accurate measure of peer delinquency by using responses directly from those peers. In the last part of this monograph, these network data permited an examination of whether the IPV within a relationship was mutual (i.e., both partners reported IPV victimization) or one-sided (i.e., only one partner within a couple reported IPV victimization). These important network data are described in further detail below.

IN-HOME INTERVIEWS

Respondents for the Add Health survey were selected using a two-stage stratified sample design. In the first stage, 132 schools were randomly selected from a national sampling pool of 26,666 high schools stratified by region, urbanicity, school size, school type (private or public), and racial composition. More than 90,000 students from the 132 selected schools completed in-school questionnaires. All students from the selected schools who had parental consent and were present on the day of the survey administration could complete the survey.

In the second stage of the data collection the sampled schools were stratified by gender and grade, and a nationally representative subsample of adolescents was selected to complete in-home interviews.

The in-home interviews were originally conducted during 1995, and they make-up the longitudinal portion of these data. Participants in the in-home interviews were re-interviewed in 1996 (Wave Two), throughout 2001 and 2002 (Wave Three), and more recently in 2007 and 2008 (wave four). A total of 20,745 respondents completed the first wave of in-home interviews, 14,728 completed the second wave of interviews, and 15,197 respondents completed the third wave of interviews. The in-home interviews had a relatively high response rate, at nearly 79% for the first wave and about 88% for the second wave.

Because the in-home interviews provide detailed information on violent offending, violent victimization, and IPV victimization, these interviews are the source of data for the present study. The in-home interviews conducted in Waves One and Two are the primary source of data for the present research, although one measure based on the Wave Three interviews is included in the analyses as well.

With the exception of the data used in Chapter 6, the sample used in this study was limited to respondents who were: (a) present in all three of the first waves of data; and, (b) reported at least one romantic or non-romantic relationship between Waves One and Two during the Wave Two interview. To make this a true study of violent offending, violent victimization, and IPV victimization among adolescents, this study was further limited to respondents who were 18-years-old or younger at the time of the second wave interview. The final sample includes a total of 6,279 respondents: 95% of these respondents were involved in a romantic relationship, and the remaining 5% were involved in a sexual relationship deemed as a romantic relationship by survey administrators (this distinction is described in greater detail below).

Although one advantage of using these data was the longitudinal design of the survey, the length of the interval between Waves One and Two was short for some respondents. The interval between the first two waves ranges from about four months to one year and four months for this sample of respondents. The average length of the interval was approximately 11 months. Separate analyses were conducted using both the entire sample of romantically involved 11 to 18-year-olds and only those respondents who had a minimum of 11 months pass between the first and second wave interviews. The results of these analyses were not significantly different; thus, the entire sample of respondents who met the above criteria were used.

Table 3.1. Definition and Calculation of Variables Included in Research

Measure	Description and Calculation
Dependent Measures	
IPV (Wave Two)	Based on five survey items, measured in two ways: binary (coded "1" if any of the items ever occurred) and variety scale (ranges from zero to five based on the number of items experienced by the respondent)
IPV - Verbal Abuse Only (Wave Two)	Based on three survey items, measured in two ways: binary (coded "1" if any of the items ever occurred) and variety scale (ranges from zero to three based on the number of items experienced by the respondent)
IPV - Physical Abuse Only (Wave Two)	Based on three survey items, measured in two ways: binary (coded "1" if any of the items ever occurred) and variety scale (ranges from zero to two based on the number of items experienced by the respondent)
Mutual IPV (Wave Two)	Binary measure coded "1" if both individuals within the couple reported any measure of IPV
One-Sided IPV (Wave Two)	Binary measure coded "1" if the respondent reported any measure of IPV but his or her partner did not
Violent Offending (Waves One and Two)	Based on five survey items, measured using a variety scale that ranges from zero to five based on the number of items experienced by the respondent within the previous 12 months
Violent Victimization (Waves One and Two)	Based on four survey items, measured using a variety scale that ranges from zero to four based on the number of items experienced by the respondent within the previous 12 months
General Delinquency (Waves One and Two)	Based on nine survey items, measured using a variety scale that ranges from zero to nine based on the number of items experienced by the respondent within the previous 12 months
Drug Use (Waves One and Two)	Binary measure coded "1" if the respondent reported use of at least one of five illicit drugs within the previous 12 months

Table 3.1. Definition and Calculation of Variables Included in Research (Continued)

Measure	Description and Calculation
Relationship Characteristics (All Wave Two)	
Duration	Continuous measure of the total duration of the relationship in years
Emotional Intensity	Standardized scale composed of ten items, including mostly non-physical activities engaged in by the couple during the relationship
Sexual Activity	Standardized scale composed of four items, including sexual behaviors engaged in by the couple during the relationship
Peer Network Measures (All Wave One)	
Mean Network Delinquency	Mean value of four minor delinquency items committed by peers in the respondent's send and receive network
Size of Peer Network	Measured by the total number of others nominated by the respondent, and the total number of others who nominated the respondent
Isolate	Binary measure coded "1" if respondent has no peers in network his or her send and receive network
In-degree	Count of the number of others who nominate respondent as a peer
Out-degree	Count of the number of others nominated by the respondent as peers
Density	Number of ties in respondent's peer network divided by the number of possible ties in the network
Bonacich Centrality	Measure of respondent's centrality in his/her network, weighted by the centrality of others in the send and receive network
Proportion Opposite Sex	Measure of the proportion of the respondent's peer network that is opposite sex
Background Measures	
Male	Binary measure of respondent sex, coded "1" if respondent is male
African American	Binary measure of respondent race, coded "1" if respondent is African American

Table 3.1. Definition and Calculation of Variables Included in Research (Continued)

Measure	Description and Calculation
Background Measures, continued	
Other Race	Binary measure of respondent race, coded "1" if respondent is not African American or White
Physical Development	Binary measure coded "1" if respondent is at or above the 50th percentile of physical development compared to other survey respondents of the same gender; measure based on four survey questions for males and three questions for females
Two-Parent Home	Binary measure coded "1" if respondent lived in a two-parent home during both waves of interviews
Age	Continuous measure of age measured in years at the time of the Wave Two interview
Family Socioeconomic Status	Standardized mean of respondent's parents' education and occupational prestige, based on questions from the Add Health parents' survey
Unstructured Socializing	Count measure of how much time respondent spends "just hanging out" with friends during the week, ranges from "0" (no time) to "3" (five or more times per week)
Drunkenness	Count measure of how often respondent gets drunk on alcohol, ranges from "0" (never) to "6" (every day or most days)
Tobacco Use	Binary measure coded "1" if respondent reported any use of tobacco products within previous 12 months
Parental Supervision	Count measure of how often mother and/or father are home when respondent leaves for school or goes to bed at night, ranges from "1" (low level of supervision) to "5" (high level of supervision)
Depression	Standardized composite of 19 survey items commonly associated with depression, ranges from "0" (low level of depression) to "3"

Table 3.1. Definition and Calculation of Variables Included in Research (Continued)

Measure	Description and Calculation
Background Measures, continued	
Self-Esteem	Standardized composite of 7 survey items commonly associated with self-esteem, ranges from "1" (low level of self-esteem) to "5" (high level of self-esteem)
School Trouble	Standardized composite of 5 survey items reflecting whether respondent gets along with others at school and/or feels safe there, ranges from "1" (low level of school trouble) to "5" (high level of school trouble)
Childhood Maltreatment (Measured at Wave Three)	Retrospective count measure of whether respondent was mistreated by parents/guardians as a child, ranges from "0" (no childhood maltreatment) to "6" (all six measures of childhood maltreatment occurred)

ROMANTIC RELATIONSHIP DATA

Respondents could report up to three romantic partners during the second wave interview, and detailed questions were asked about each relationship. About 52% of the sample reported at least one relationship, and only data from the first relationship were used in this study. A majority of the respondents who had at least one romantic relationship had only one relationship (63%). Respondents were asked several questions about each romantic partnership, including when each relationship began and ended, the age and grade of each partner, and whether each partner ever verbally or physically abused the respondent.

In a separate section of questions, respondents were asked whether they had a physical relationship with another person, not including any person reported as a romantic partner in the section described above. If the respondent answered "yes" to this question, three additional questions were asked to determine whether this physical "non-romantic" relationship was actually a romantic relationship. Respondents were asked whether they have ever done the following three things with their non-romantic partner: (1) held hands; (2) kissed on the mouth; and, (3) told the partner that they liked or loved him or her. If the respondent answered yes to all three of these questions, the non-romantic relationship was considered a romantic relationship. In these cases the respondent was asked a series of questions about this non-romantic partner identical to the questions asked about romantic partners. Respondents could report up to three non-romantic relationships, and approximately 15% of respondents reported at least one non-romantic relationship.

When listing romantic and non-romantic partners, respondents could identify their partners from the list of other respondents. If the identified partners participated in the second wave of interviews, couples could be matched and data could be extracted from both partners within the couple. These matched couples comprise the secure romantic relationship data used in Chapter 6. A total of 865 couples could be matched, but only 220 of these partners were mutually reciprocated. In other words, for only 220 of these relationships did each partner within the couple identify the other as a partner.

Because this section of analyses relied upon having complete information about the relationship from both individuals within the relationship, only the 220 reciprocated partnerships could be used. With so few respondents (440 individuals), having complete information on all of the variables was crucial. Thus, multiple imputation was used for these data (described below).

PEER NETWORK DATA

To examine how friendship networks influence behavior, this study employed the Add Health peer network data. During the first and second wave interviews, respondents were asked to identify their five best male and five best female friends from a roster of students in their schools. If a nominated peer's name did not appear on the roster, students were asked whether this friend: (a) attended the same school and was not listed for some reason; (b) attended a participating feeder middle school; or, (c) did not attend either the respondent's school or the participating feeder middle schools. Approximately 13% of all peers who were nominated could not be identified and matched to the respondent. With these data, it is possible to create measures of the structural characteristics of the friendship networks (e.g., the size and density of the peer network) and to directly measure the delinquency of the peer networks based on responses from the peers. These network data allow researchers to take responses directly from identified peers and to measure the structural properties of respondents' peer networks.

MEASURES

Intimate Partner Violence

Victimization by an intimate partner during adolescence was the key variable in this study. In the first part (Chapter 4), past violent offending and violent victimization were used to predict abuse by an intimate partner. In the second part (Chapter 5), IPV victimization was used to predict violent offending, violent victimization, delinquency, and drug use.

Add Health captured intimate partner abuse with five questions, which include both non-physical and physical forms of abuse. These questions were asked only of respondents who reported at least one romantic or non-romantic relationship since the first wave interview (an average of 11 months passed between Waves One and Two). The following five questions were used to measure intimate partner abuse for both romantic and non-romantic relationships:

1) Did your partner call you names, insult you, or treat you disrespectfully in front of others?
2) Did your partner swear at you?
3) Did your partner threaten you with violence?
4) Did your partner push or shove you?
5) Did your partner throw something at you that could hurt you?

Respondents who completed this portion of the questionnaire could answer "yes" (this event occurred), "no" (this event did not occur), or "I don't know." They could also refuse to answer this question. Fewer than 0.002% of respondents who were involved in relationships refused to answer each of the five partner abuse questions or responded with "I don't know."

These dichotomous measures were used to construct three scales: (1) a scale that represents all five partner abuse measures; (2) a scale that includes only the three verbal abuse measures; and, (3) a scale that includes only the two physical abuse items. Dichotomized versions of these scales are also included to use with logistic regression. During Wave Two interviews, approximately 28% of the sample answered "yes" to at least one of the partner abuse questions, 26% reported at least one verbal abuse measure, and about 9% reported at least one physical abuse measure. A description of these three measures can be found in Table 3.1.

Mutual and One-sided IPV Victimization

The purpose of using the matched network relationships was to see whether one or both partners reported IPV within the relationship. If both partners reported IPV, then the IPV was probably mutual and resembles what Johnson (2008) calls situational couple violence. If only one individual within the partnership reported IPV, then the IPV was one-sided and resembles what Johnson calls intimate terrorism. If both partners within the couple reported IPV, then a dichotomous variable was created to indicate mutual IPV for both individuals in the couple. If only one partner within a couple reported IPV, a dichotomous variable was created for the victim only (not the other partner within the couple).

Violent Offending and Violent Victimization

In addition to partner abuse victimization, violent offending and violent victimization were both key measures in this research. Both were used as primary independent measures in Chapter 4, and dependent measures in Chapter 5. Wave One versions of these measures were used as independent variables in the first section of analyses (Chapter 4), and both Wave One and Two versions of these measures were used in the second section of analyses (Chapter 5).

To measure violent offending, a variety scale was created (described below) using five questions. In both Waves One and Two, respondents were asked how often in the past 12 months did they commit each of the following offenses:

1) You got into a serious physical fight?
2) You hurt someone badly enough to need bandages or care

from a doctor or nurse?
3) You pulled a knife or gun on someone?
4) You shot or stabbed someone?
5) You used or threatened to use a weapon to get something from someone?

For items 1, 2, and 5, respondents could select one of the following answers for each question: (1) never, (2) one or two times, (3) three or four times, (4) five or more times. For items 3 and 4, respondents could respond with (1) this event never occurred, (2) this event occurred once, or (3) this event occurred more than once. For all items the respondents could also choose not to answer the question or respond with "I don't know." For all of the above items, fewer than 0.01% of respondents refused to answer the questions or responded with "I don't know."

Violent victimization was also measured using a variety scale based on answers to four questions. Respondents were asked how many times in the past 12 months they experienced each of the following events:

1) You were in a physical fight in which you were injured and had to be treated by a doctor or nurse?
2) Someone shot you?
3) Someone cut or stabbed you?
4) You were jumped?

The first violent victimization item was a continuous measure and respondents could report 0 to 333 occurrences of this event. The remaining three items could be answered with one of the following responses: (1) this event never occurred; (2) this event occurred once; or, (3) this event occurred more than one time. For all items, respondents could also refuse to answer these questions or they could respond with "I don't know." Fewer than 0.01% of respondents chose one of the last two responses.

The violent victimization index could have been confounded with partner abuse because the survey questions did not identify the attacker (e.g., whether the respondent knew the perpetrator, whether the attacker was a friend or intimate partner). However, the wording of the general violence questions does not make it likely that the respondents confused these questions with partner abuse victimization.

Both the violent offending and violent victimization scales are *variety scales*, indexes which consist of the sum of dichotomized measures. The use of variety scales can correct for some of the common problems associated with traditional self-report scales for crime and delinquency. Such scales have become common for self-report measures of crime since Nye and Short (1957) demonstrated the usefulness of delinquency scales over half a century ago. Traditional self-report scales consist of the sum of multiple measures that reflect how often individuals engaged in each delinquent act (e.g., the number of times an adolescent engaged in retail theft added to the number of times an adolescent painted graffiti). Thus, they capture frequency across many different acts of delinquency.

Self-report scales are useful for three reasons (Nunnally 1978; see also Osgood, McMorris, and Potenza 2002). First, self-report scales can represent the constructs of crime and delinquency more completely than a single item, and the combination of items can reduce the idiosyncratic error that comes with any particular item. Second, scales can increase the reliability and precision of a measurement. Finally, so the combination of multiple items can make a measurement that is more continuous, even though most measurements of delinquency come with only a few response categories.

Despite the benefits of these scales, self-report scales nonetheless have some problems. Using traditional delinquency scales with ordinary regression techniques may represent a problem because the distribution of these scales is usually not normal. The mode for each type of offending behavior is usually zero, although a very small proportion of respondents have probably engaged in several acts of deviance many times (Osgood et al. 2002). Most summative self-report scales violate the assumption of equal intervals in two ways: (1) the seriousness of offenses varies within scales; and, (2) the frequency of offending varies across each item within a scale. Although the central limit theorem dictates that measures will group around the mean and create a normal distribution and that the sum of measures will do the same, this theorem does not hold true for measures of offending. Rather than appearing to be continuous, normally distributed, and symmetrical, the distribution of summative self-report scales tends to be "limited, discrete, and skewed" (Osgood et al. 2002, 270).

Item response theory (IRT) has been proposed as a solution to this common problem. For measures of self-reported offending, IRT scaling corrects for scales that consist of (a) serious and less serious items and (b) items for which the modal response is zero (Osgood et al. 2002). In brief, the process of IRT scaling starts with a construct (in this case, delinquency) that is assumed to be continuous, with equal intervals and perfect measurement. Rather than adding the multiple delinquency items together, IRT scaling uses a maximum likelihood model to determine the respondents' positions on the underlying construct based on how they responded to the multiple delinquency items.

While IRT has proven to produce more accurate scales than traditional scaling techniques, the process of IRT scaling is extremely complex and cumbersome. Thus, the present study employed variety scales which can approximate scales produced by IRT scaling. Variety scales are similar to the commonly used summative scales, except each item is recoded to zero for an act that never happened, and one for an act that happened one or more times. Next, all of the dichotomized items are added together. When used with tobit, Poisson, or negative binomial regression, variety scales can act as a proxy for IRT scaling. The analytic strategy adopted here is described in more detail later in this chapter.

Delinquency

Both Wave One and Wave Two measures of adolescent offending were used in the analyses. For both waves, adolescent offending was measured using a nine-item variety scale. Respondents were asked how often in the previous 12 months they committed each of the following acts:

1) Paint graffiti or signs on someone else's property or in a public space?
2) Deliberately damage property that didn't belong to you?
3) Take something from a store without paying for it?
4) Run away from home?
5) Drive a car without permission from its owner?
6) Steal something worth less than $50?

    7) Steal something worth more than $50?
    8) Go into a house or building and steal something?
    9) Sell marijuana or other drugs?

    Respondents could respond with one of the following answers: (1) never; (2) one or two times; (3) three or four times; or, (4) five or more times. Respondents could also refuse to answer these questions, or respond with "I don't know," options taken by fewer than 0.01% of respondents. Each of these responses was dichotomized and all of the responses were added together to create a variety scale.

Drug Use
Whether the respondent reported drug use during the second wave interview was a primary dependent variable in Chapters 5 and 6. A Wave One measure of drug use was also used in these analyses to control for prior use. In the first wave interview, respondents were asked whether and how often they used any of the following drugs: (1) marijuana; (2) cocaine; (3) ecstasy (MDMA); (4) LSD; and, (5) illicit intravenous drugs. In the second wave, respondents were asked whether they used any of the above drugs since the previous interview. For both waves, a dichotomous measure of whether the respondent used any of these drugs was used. Marijuana was the most commonly reported drug, with about 26% of respondents reporting use between the first and second wave interviews. Much like the other measures described above, drug use had a very low frequency of refusals or reports of "I don't know," with fewer than 0.02% of respondents choosing to answer with either of these options. All of the above measures are described in Table 3.1.

Relationship Characteristics
The analyses also included characteristics of the romantic relationships, including the length of the relationships, the emotional intensity shared in relationships, and the amount of sexual activity experienced during the relationships.

    The duration of the relationship was measured in months, with respondents reporting the month and year that the relationship began and ended. Unfortunately, this measure had a relatively high rate of missingness because several respondents either refused to provide this information, they could not recall this information, or this information was missing for another reason. Most of the non-responses came from respondents being unable to recall this information. Approximately 13% of the respondents used in this study could not provide the length of their relationships. To address the high rate of missing data for this and other measures multiple imputation was used, an analytic technique which is described in further detail below.

Both the emotional intensity and the sexual activity measures were based on a set of 15 cards presented to respondents which contained information on various activities that could have occurred during the relationship (e.g., the couple exchanged presents, met each other's parents). Respondents were asked to keep the cards that contained activities that occurred during the relationship, and set aside events that did not occur. Thus, the respondents could either accept the cards or reject the cards, creating a binary response.

Based on the results of an exploratory factor analysis on these cards, identical to the factor analysis used by McCarthy and Casey (2008) on these measures, two scales of emotional intensity and sexual activity were created from these cards. A tetrachoric factor analysis, which is well-suited for dichotomous measures, was used to identify two unique constructs (indicated by eigenvalues of 1 or greater).

The emotional intensity measure was an additive composite indicating in how many of the following ten items the couple engaged (eigenvalue = 8.73): they went out with a group, saw other friends less, went out alone, met each other's parents, were seen as a couple by others, held hands, exchanged presents, expressed love to one another, thought of themselves as a couple, and kissed. The sexual activity scale indicated in how many of the following four items the couple engaged (eigenvalue = 1.47): they talked about contraceptives, touched each other under their clothes, touched each other's genitals, and had sexual intercourse. A description of all of these variables can be found in Table 3.1, and a list of the factor loadings for these two variables is listed in Table 3.2.

Peer Network Measures

Nine variables from the peer network data were used in this study. The first two were measures of the average delinquency and violence in the respondent's peer network. These measures were based on responses to survey questions both from friends nominated by the respondent and from friends who nominated the respondent (i.e., the respondent's send and receive network). Peer network delinquency and violence measures were based on responses to the in-school questionnaire administered during the first wave of the study. To measure delinquency, the in-school questionnaire asked respondents how often they engaged in each of the following acts: smoked cigarettes, drank alcohol, got drunk from alcohol, and skipped school. To measure violence, the in-school questionnaire asked respondents how often they had been involved in a serious physical fight within the previous 12 months. Responses ranged from zero (indicating never) to four (indicating more than seven times). For both measures of delinquency and of violence, responses for all of the peers in the send and receive network were added and then divided by the total number of peers in this network.

In addition to measures of peer delinquency and violence, this study also included seven measures of peer network structural characteristics that captured the size of the respondent's peer network, the popularity of the respondent, and the gender composition of the respondent's peer network. The size of the respondent's network was measured using two variables: total network size and whether or not the respondent is an isolate. The network size measure represented the total number of individuals in the respondent's peer group (both peers nominated by the respondent, and peers who nominated the respondent as a friend). The second measure of network size was a dichotomous measure that represented whether the respondent had no friendship ties. In other words, the respondent did not identify anyone as a friend, and no one participating in the survey identified the respondent as a friend (coded "1" if the respondent was an isolate).

The popularity of the respondent was captured using four measures. The first two popularity measures were the in-degree and out-degree variables. The in-degree measure reflected the number of others who nominated the respondent as a friend. This measure is generally regarded as a crude measure of popularity. The out-degree measure reflected the number of peers nominated by the respondent, and is generally regarded as a measure of peer influence.

The third and fourth measures of respondent popularity were the density and centrality measures. Network density was based on the number of friendship ties in the respondent's local peer network divided by the number of possible ties in the entire school's network. The centrality measure (i.e., the Bonacich power centrality index) captured the in-degree and out-degree network of both the respondent and of other peer group members to whom the respondent was connected. The centrality measure reflected how central the respondent was in his or her peer network, or if the respondent was on the periphery of the network. Adolescents who were more central in their peer networks were regarded as more active in the peer networks, and were likely more susceptible to the norms and expectations of this network.

Table 3.2. Factor Loadings for Emotional Intensity and Sexual Activity Items

Measure	Description	Factor Loading	Uniqueness
Emotional	Out with group	0.68	0.53
Intensity	Saw friends less	0.67	0.56
	Went out alone	0.79	0.38
	Met parents	0.79	0.38
	Seen as couple	0.88	0.22
	Held hands	0.95	0.11
	Exchanged presents	0.79	0.37
	Expressed love	0.79	0.38
	Identified as couple	0.90	0.18
	Kissed	0.89	0.21
Sexual	Talked about contraceptives	0.73	0.47
Activity	Touched under clothes	0.97	0.05
	Touched genitals	0.97	0.07
	Had sexual intercourse	0.91	0.17

The final measure of the respondent's peer network was the proportion of his or network composed of opposite sex friends. This measure was created by, first, measuring the number of female and male friends in the send and receive network and, second, dividing each measure by the total number of ties in the respondent's network. This created two measures that reflected the proportion of the respondent's friends who were male and the proportion of the respondent's friends who were female. If the respondent were male, the proportion of the respondent's network that was female was inserted as their proportion of opposite sex friends measure. If the respondent were female, the proportion of the respondent's network that was male was inserted as their proportion of opposite sex friends measure.

As indicated above, all of the peer network measures had a high rate of missing data. Rather than omit cases that had missing network data, multiple imputation was used to address the missing data. This missing data estimation method is described in further detail below.

Other Control Measures

This study also employed several basic control variables, including gender (a dummy variable representing male respondents, using female respondents as the reference category), age (continuous, measured in years), race (two dummy variables that represented African Americans and other races; white respondents comprised the reference category), and family structure (whether the respondent lived with both parents during both Waves One and Two). The household's socio-economic status (SES) was measured using a standardized mean of parental occupational prestige and parental education based on the questionnaire filled out by the parents of the respondent.

A measure of the respondent's physical development during Wave Two was also used. As described in Chapter 1, physical development can have a significant influence on delinquency, especially for adolescent females (Zahn et al. 2010). This measure was based on a standardized, composite index of four items for males and three items for females reflecting how physically developed respondents rated themselves. Respondents who scored in the 50th percentile or higher were coded as one (more physically developed), and those who scored below the 50th percentile were coded as zero (less physically developed).

Given that limited adult supervision and time spent with peers in the absence of adults are both related to delinquency (Osgood et al. 1996), the analyses also included measures of parental supervision and unstructured socializing. Parental supervision was a four-item scale that represented how often the respondent's mother and/or father were home when the respondent left for school each morning and went to bed at night. The unstructured socializing measure was based on a question that asked the respondent how much time they spent "just hanging out" each week.

Because depression has been shown to have a strong relationship to both offending (Beyers and Loeber 2003) and victimization (Sweeting et al. 2006), a scale of depressive symptoms was included in all of the analyses. Self-esteem, drunkenness (a measure of how often the respondent gets drunk or very high), drug use (identical to the measure described earlier), and tobacco were also used as controls in the analyses.

Finally, the models also controlled for parental maltreatment. Parental maltreatment measures were captured using retrospective questioning during the third wave. Respondents were asked whether any of the following happened during their childhoods: (1) left home alone before grade 6; (2) deprived of basic necessities; (3) slapped, hit, or kicked; (4) sexually abused; (5) home investigated by social services; and, (5) taken out of the home by social services. Including the third wave did not result in significant data loss. All of these measures were included in a scale. A description of all of the above variables can be found in Table 3.1.

MULTIPLE IMPUTATION

Because some of the key variables in these analyses had a high rate of missing data, multiple imputation was used to correct for the missing data. The variables that had the most missing data included the duration of the relationship measure and all nine of the peer network measures. Multiple imputation was also used for many of the measures in the reciprocated romantic nominations dataset. Given the small size of this dataset, even a small number of missing cases could have been problematic. Missing data can be problematic for analyses because it can produce biased coefficients, which in turn can lead to invalid conclusions. Missing data can also reduce or inflate statistical power (Acock 2005).

There are three major categories of missing data: missing completely at random (MCAR), missing at random (MAR), and non-ignorable (NI) missing data. When missing data are MCAR, missing values are randomly distributed throughout the data; the pattern of missingness does not follow a systematic pattern. This category of missing data rarely occurs in the social sciences, and any assumption of MCAR data can usually not be met.

Data are MAR if the observed missingness pattern does not depend on the values that are unobserved (Heitjan and Basu 1996). In other words, the pattern of missing data is not related to the outcome measure after controlling for the other observed variables in the study. Missing data are NI when the pattern of missingness is systematic and related to the outcome measure. Control measures cannot account for the effect of missing data. Missing data are especially problematic when they are NI, as they can create biased coefficients.

To use multiple imputation, we must assume that the pattern of missing data for the most affected variables (i.e., relationship duration and peer network measures) is either MCAR or MAR. The assumption of MCAR is nearly impossible to meet, while MAR is a more reasonable assumption. It is probable that the patterns of missing data for duration and peer network characteristics were MAR. The pattern of missing data for relationship duration was likely related to the respondents' abilities to recall date information. It is possible that the longest and shortest relationships had the highest rate of missing data, but this pattern was probably not related to any of the outcomes of interest (e.g., IPV victimization, violent offending).

The missingness of the network measures was mostly based on the ability of the survey administrators to identify and match peer nominations to respondents. About 13% of all peer nominations went unmatched. Of this 13%, about 15% were left unmatched because the nominated peers went to a school that was not participating in the Add Health study, and 8% of these unmatched peers were due to the nominated peer's name not appearing on the school roster. It is unlikely that this pattern of missingness was due to a systematic bias.

Multiple imputation is a maximum likelihood approach to missing data that creates multiple data sets in which missing values are replaced with maximum likelihood values. For each new data set, the replacement values are based on all of the observed measures and relationships among these measures. Missing values are replaced throughout multiple iterations until successive iterations are sufficiently similar. In other words, when the covariance matrix begins to look identical to previous iterations, the iterative process stops (Acock 2005, 1,019). This pattern is repeated for a specified number of datasets (in this case, five). With each new data set and iterative process, a degree of random error is injected to reflect the uncertainty of the imputation and the imperfection of this process. Each set of data created is slightly different than the dataset before it. Once the multiple (five) data sets are completed, the parameters can be averaged. The uncertainty about the missing data and the precision of the imputation process is reflected in the standard errors. In the present study, the ICE command in Stata (version 11) was used to impute missing data. Five new stacked datasets were created.

ANALYTIC PLAN

The results of this study are presented in the next three chapters. Each set of results begins with a basic descriptive account of the analyzed data, followed by a multivariate analysis of the data. In order to maximize the number of respondents that could be used in this study, the data and analyses were divided into two main sections. These two sections of data and analyses are described below.

Section One

The first section of data consisted of all respondents from the in-home interviews who were present for all three waves of data, were involved in at least one romantic or non-romantic relationship between Waves One and Two, and who were 18-years-old or younger at the time of Wave Two. This first section of data was used in Chapters 4 and 5.

Both Chapters 4 and 5 begin with simple descriptive accounts of the phenomena that were analyzed. In Chapter 4, the extent to which

Wave One violent offending and violent victimization and Wave Two IPV victimization overlapped is examined. In this chapter, the prevalence of Wave One violent offending and violent victimization among respondents who have and have not been victimized by a romantic partner is examined first. This chapter also reveals how often these occurrences overlapped in the data (i.e., how often individuals report Wave One violent offending and violent victimization and Wave Two IPV victimization). The extent to which these phenomena are correlated is also examined. Then the overlap between violent offending, violent victimization, and IPV victimization are examined relative to peer network measures. In addition, gender differences are examined.

In Chapter 5, the relationship between Wave Two IPV victimization and Wave Two violent offending, violent victimization, delinquency, and drug use net of prior behaviors is examined. The prevalence of Wave Two violent offending, violent victimization, delinquency, and drug use among victims of IVP is first examined. Then, these relationships are compared across male and female victims of IPV. The Add Health survey did not measure IPV victimization at Wave One, so it was not possible to include this measure in any of the models.

In both Chapters 4 and 5, the bivariate descriptions of these data are followed by the multivariate analyses. All of the multivariate analyses were conducted using Stata (version 11) and the survey-set option within Stata. The survey-set command fitted the statistical models analyzed in this study to the complex design and the correlated error structure of the Add Health data. The "mim" command was also utilized in these analyses in order to converge all five of the datasets created using multiple imputation.

The analyses used design weights to ensure that each population was represented appropriately in the analyses. That is, certain populations (e.g., racial/ethnic minority groups, economically disadvantaged groups) were over-sampled to ensure that they would be included in the data, and design weights allowed the analyses to accurately reflect how much of the population each group should actually represented.

Logistic regression was used to predict the occurrence of IPV victimization in Chapter 4. Logistic regression was the most appropriate form of regression for these analyses, given the binary nature of the dependent variable, IPV victimization. The measures of IPV victimization in Add Health measured only the types of abuse (i.e., three forms of verbal abuse and two forms of physical abuse) and not the frequency of abuse. Most of the sample (about 72%) reported no IPV victimization. Of those respondents who reported any IPV victimization, a majority (16% out of 28%) reported only one type of IPV victimization. Probability models, such as logistic regression, are best for binary data. With binary outcomes, the error term is necessarily heteroscedastic. Using ordinary least squares regression to predict such outcomes is inefficient and creates biased coefficients (Liao 1994).

Negative binomial regression was used to predict violent offending, violent victimization, and delinquency in Chapter 5. Both violent offending and delinquency were measured using variety scales. As described above, variety scales that are analyzed by tobit, Poisson, or negative binomial regression approximate IRT scaling. The measures of violent offending, violent victimization, and delinquency were over-dispersed. That is, the variances of these outcomes exceeded the means. Thus, negative binomial regression was the most appropriate analytic tool for these data.

Also in Chapter 5, logistic regression was used once again to predict drug use. Much like IPV victimization, drug use in this sample also had a binary distribution. Most of the respondents (79%) did not use any drugs. Of those respondents who reported illicit drug use, most used only one drug (typically only marijuana). Very few of the respondents reported use of cocaine (<2%), inhalants (1%), or psychedelic drugs (<4%).

Section Two

The purpose of these analyses was to determine whether different types of partner violence (mutual versus one-sided partner violence) had different risk factors (predictors) and outcomes (e.g., violent offending, delinquency, and drug use).

The network couple data were used in two ways in Chapter 6. In the first set of analyses, the couple data were analyzed at the couple level. That is, the data were arranged so that each couple occupied a single line of data. Thus, there were a total of 220 cases which contained information for both the male and female partners. This version of the data was analyzed using multinomial regression. The outcomes were dichotomous measures of whether the couple experienced mutual IPV or one-sided IPV. Couples who did not experience any form of IPV served as the reference category. These analyses are described in more detail in Chapter 6.

For the next set of analyses, the couple data were analyzed at both the individual and couple level. That is, the data occupied two levels. The first level of data was arranged so that each of the 440 individuals occupied a single line of data. Relationship characteristics (e.g., duration, sexual activity) occupied the second level of data. Thus, there were 220 level-two units (the couples) and 440 individual-level units. Because these data are nested, this version of the data was analyzed using multi-level modeling in Hierarchical Linear and Non-Linear Modeling software (HLM version 6). HLM is ideal for these analyses because it can provide better estimates for these nested data than regular individual-level models. These better estimates come from the fact that similar estimates exist for other similar couples. This statistical software is also suited for analyzing multiply imputed data by combining the newly created datasets for analysis.

Because there are similarities among individuals who are linked in a romantic relationship, nested data violate two common assumptions of regression techniques—namely the assumption of independence and the assumption of homoscedasticity. The assumption of independence refers to the stipulation that error terms should not be correlated with one another. The nested nature of these data violates that assumption because individual respondents are nested within larger groups (i.e., couples). Individuals nested within the same couples are probably more like one another, increasing the likelihood that the error terms are correlated. Given that data are almost never measured perfectly, there is likely to be error due to omitted variable bias, and this bias is similar for respondents located in the same schools and communities. Thus, the error terms are likely to be correlated.

The violation of homoscedasticity happens when the variance is not constant across the regression line. In other words, there is very little variance at one end of the regression line but high variance at the other end of the regression line (presumably at the higher values). This is a problem because it means that there is less error when predicting lower values than when predicting higher values of some given variable (especially true for delinquency).

When these two assumptions are violated, the analyses assume more power than what actually exists. For example, the second arrangement of the network romantic partner data used in this research has 440 cases at the individual level, but at the macro-level (i.e., couple-level) each of those cases has the same value on contextual variables (i.e., couple-level characteristics). So, although it may appear that the analyses have a reasonable amount of statistical power, the secure romantic relationship data only have half of that power. These problems can be corrected by using multilevel modeling techniques (HLM). Analyses that address the violations described above produce the same results as analyses that do not correct for these problems; however, the corrected analyses produce larger standard errors and more accurate significance tests.

Using HLM for the second version of the couple data, the analyses conducted in Chapter 5 were replicated. Rather than being an individual-level predictor, IPV victimization was a level-two couple characteristic. This measure was represented using three level-two binary measures: (1) mutual IPV, (2) one-sided IPV with a female victim, and (3) one-sided IPV with a male victim. These analyses are described in considerable detail in Chapter 6.

CHAPTER 4

Adolescent Intimate Partner Violence Risk Factors

INTRODUCTION

In this chapter, two main questions are addressed. First, to what extent do prior violent offending, violent victimization, and intimate partner violence victimization overlap? In other words, does the same victim-offender overlap that applies to general delinquency and violent offending extend to IPV victimization? Second, are prior violent offending and violent victimization predictive of IPV victimization?

In addition to answering the above questions, this section also examines the roles of peer networks and gender in these relationships. Prior research on IPV victimization has not considered whether or how peer networks influence this type of victimization. Also, because prior research on this topic has focused almost exclusively on female victims of IPV, these results also examine males and females separately to look for any possible similarities and differences in how both genders experience IPV victimization.

The analyses and results presented in this chapter are divided into three main sections. First, this chapter provides a description of the sample and measures used in these analyses. Second, the bivariate relationships are presented and discussed. In the final section of this chapter, the multivariate results are presented and discussed. In this section, several factors, including Wave One violent offending and violent victimization, were used to predict Wave Two IPV victimization.

THE SAMPLE AND DESCRIPTIVE STATISTICS

The data used in this section include respondents who met the following criteria: (a) they were included in the first three waves of interviews; (b) they were involved in at least one romantic or non-romantic relationship during the second wave interview; and, (c) they were between the ages of 11 and 18 at the time of the second interview.

Tables 4.1 and 4.2 provide a description of the 6,279 respondents included in this sample. Table 4.1 includes the descriptive statistics for the measures of all violence (both partner and non-partner-related) in Waves One and Two. As can be seen in this table, the respondents engaged in an average of 0.68 violent offenses (not IPV-related) during Wave One and even fewer (0.44) during Wave Two. The respondents were victimized by an average of 0.55 aggressive acts in the year preceding Wave One and 0.26 violent victimizations between the first and second wave interviews. Overall, respondents engaged in and were victims of fewer violent acts in Wave Two. The decline in violence between Waves One and Two is likely due to "telescoping" (Shaffer and Ruback 2002). That is, during the first wave interview respondents likely reported events that occurred outside of the period about which they were questioned. During the second wave interview, the first wave interview probably provided an anchor or recognizable time point from which to report incidents (Cook and Campbell 1979).

Based on the binary measures of Wave Two IPV victimization, also listed in Table 4.1, about 27% of the respondents reported being the victims of IPV (either verbal or physical). About 25% of this sample reported at least one instance of verbal intimidation, and 9% reported being the victims of at least one physical assault by their intimate partners. These estimates are consistent with reports from the CDC described in Chapter 1, although they are slightly lower. The count measures of IPV victimization, also listed in Table 4.1, reveal that the respondents reported experiencing less than one instance of IPV victimization (any, verbal, or physical) on average.

Table 4.1. Descriptive Statistics for Violent Offending, Violent Victimization and IPV Victimization Measures

Variable	Mean/ Percent	Std Dev	Range
Violent Offending			
Wave One Violent Offending	0.68	1.01	0 - 5
Wave Two Violent Offending	0.44	0.91	0 - 5
Violent Victimization			
Wave One Violent Victimization	0.44	0.91	0 - 4
Wave Two Violent Victimization	0.26	0.67	0 - 4
Wave Two IPV Victimization – Count			
Any Abuse	0.46	0.94	0 - 5
Verbal Abuse	0.36	0.70	0 - 3
Physical Abuse	0.10	0.36	0 - 2
Wave Two IPV Victimization - Binary			
Any Abuse	27%	--	--
Verbal Abuse	25%	--	--
Physical Abuse	9%	--	--

N = 6,279

A descriptive account of the control measures used in the analyses is displayed in Table 4.2. Forty-five percent of this sample is male and 56% are white; about 20% of the respondents are African American and 24% report other non-white races and ethnicities. The respondents range in age from 11 to 18-years-of-age, and the average age is just over 16.

Based on the relationship characteristics displayed in Table 4.2, the average duration of these relationships is surprisingly long at 12.6 months (1.05 years). Even though the average duration may seem long for adolescents, Carver et al. (2003) found that about 60% of adolescent relationships last for one year or longer, with older adolescents averaging longer relationships compared to younger adolescents. Of the ten possible non-sexual activities the respondents could have engaged in with their partners (e.g., meet each other's parents, exchange gifts), they engaged in an average of 6.03 of these activities. Respondents engaged in about 2 of the 4 possible sexual activities on average (e.g., talk about contraceptives, touched each other's genitals).

Table 4.2. Descriptive Statistics for Control Variables

Variable	Mean/ Percent	Std Dev	Range
Background Measures			
Male	45%		
African American	20%		
Other Race	24%		
Physical Development	50%		
Two-Parent Home	65%		
Drug Use	21%		
Age (In Years, Wave Two)	16.24	1.40	11 - 18
Family Socioeconomic Status	2.96	1.32	0 - 5
Unstructured Socializing	2.12	0.92	0 - 3
Drunkenness	0.85	1.41	0 - 6
Tobacco Use	6.53	11.27	0 - 30
Childhood Maltreatment	0.88	1.11	0 - 6
Parental Supervision	3.66	1.04	1 - 5
Depression	0.61	0.41	0 - 3
Self-Esteem	4.14	0.58	1 - 5
School Trouble	2.45	0.73	1 - 5
Relationship Characteristics			
Duration (In Years)	1.05	1.20	0 - 6.83
Emotional Intensity	6.03	2.34	0 - 10
Sexual Activity	1.81	1.48	0 - 4
Peer Network Measures			
Mean Network Delinquency	0.90	0.65	0 - 5
Mean Network Violence	0.75	0.55	0 - 4
Size of Peer Network	8.79	4.58	0 - 33
Isolate	4%	0.21	
In-degree	5.11	3.88	0 - 30
Out-degree	4.73	2.93	0 - 10
Density	0.30	0.18	0 - 1
Bonacich Centrality	0.89	0.64	0 - 5
Proportion Opposite Sex	0.44	0.24	0 - 1

N = 6,279

The average delinquency of the respondents' peer networks ranged from zero (no peers reported delinquent acts) to five (all of the respondents' peers engaged in all five of the possible delinquent acts). On average, most of the respondents' peers engaged in few delinquent acts (0.90). The peer networks included in these analyses also had a low level of violent offending (i.e., how often they reported involvement in fights within the previous year). The respondents' peer networks averaged less than one fight per year.

Very few of the respondents had no friends (i.e., they did not nominate any peers and they were not nominated by other respondents in the study). A total of 4% had no friends in their send and receive networks, and the respondents had an average of about 9 friends in their peer networks. The respondents were nominated (in-degree) and nominated (out-degree) an average of about five peers, and the respondents had an average of 30% of the possible peer ties that they could have had (density). The respondents also had mostly same-sex friendships, although on average about 44% of their networks were composed of opposite sex friends.

BIVARIATE RESULTS: THE PREVALENCE OF VIOLENT OFFENDING, VIOLENT VICTIMIZATION, AND IPV VICTIMIZATION

Displayed in Table 4.3 are the correlation coefficients between Wave One violent offending and violent victimization and all three measures of Wave Two IPV victimization. As can be seen in this table, Wave One violence (both violent offending and victimization) is significantly correlated with all three measures of Wave Two IPV victimization. According to Cohen's (1988) standards for Pearson's r correlations, the magnitude of these correlations are small. Generally, Pearson's r correlations below 0.50 are considered small. Although all of these correlations are significant with probability values less than 0.001, the magnitude of these coefficients do not imply that prior violence and IPV victimization are highly correlated (Rosenthal, Rosnow, and Rubin 2000).

Table 4.3. Correlation Coefficients—Violent Offending, Violent
Victimization, IPV Victimization

Wave Two Measure of IPV Victimization	Wave One Violence	
	Violent Offending	Violent Victimization
Any Abuse	0.11**	0.11**
Verbal Abuse	0.10**	0.11**
Physical Abuse	0.09**	0.10**

Displaying Pearson's r Correlations
N = 6,279
* p<.05, ** p<.01, *** p<.001

Tables 4.4 and 4.5 describe the prevalence of Wave One violent offending and violent victimization with Wave Two IPV victimization. These frequencies represent how often prior violent offending and violent victimization overlapped with Wave Two IPV victimization. The purpose of these tables is to gain an understanding of how often these phenomena co-occur.

First, looking at Table 4.4, we observe that out of the 27% of respondents in this sample who experienced some type of IPV victimization, about half (13%) also engaged in violent offending. This pattern is consistent across all three measures of IPV victimization. About half of victims of verbal intimidation (12% out of 25%) also engaged in violent offending, and about half of victims of physical abuse (5% out of 9%) also engaging in violent offending. The difference between these groups is statistically significant. The premise of the present study is that, just as there is an overlap between perpetrators and victims of general violence, there is also an overlap between victims of this particular type of violence (IPV) and general violent offending. These bivariate descriptions support this premise.

Table 4.4. Prevalence of Wave One Violent Offending and Wave Two
IPV Victimization

	Percentage of Adolescents Reporting:	
	No – Any IPV Victimization	Yes – Any IPV Victimization
No - Wave One Offending	46%	14%
Yes - Wave One Offending	27%	13%
Phi Coefficient	0.11**	
	No – Verbal IPV Victimization	Yes – Verbal IPV Victimization
No - Wave One Offending	47%	13%
Yes - Wave One Offending	28%	12%
Phi Coefficient	0.10**	
	No – Physical IPV Victim.	Yes – Physical IPV Victim.
No - Wave One Offending	56%	4%
Yes - Wave One Offending	35%	5%
Phi Coefficient	0.09**	

N = 6,263
Difference between groups significant at *p < 0.01, **Difference between groups significant at p < 0.001

Table 4.5. Prevalence of Wave One Violent Victimization and Wave Two IPV Victimization

	Percentage of Adolescents Reporting:	
	No – Any IPV Victimization	Yes – Any IPV Victimization
No - Wave One Victimization	47%	14%
Yes - Wave One Victimization	26%	13%
Phi Coefficient	0.11*	
	No – Verbal IPV Victimization	Yes – Verbal IPV Victimization
No - Wave One Victimization	48%	13%
Yes - Wave One Victimization	27%	12%
Phi Coefficient	0.10*	
	No – Physical IPV Victim.	Yes – Physical IPV Victim.
No - Wave One Victimization	57%	4%
Yes - Wave One Victimization	34%	5%
Phi Coefficient	0.10*	

N = 6,262
Difference between groups significant at *p < 0.01, **Difference between groups significant at p < 0.001

In Table 4.5 we observe that violent victimization also overlaps with IPV victimization. Nearly half of the respondents (47%) have not been the victim of either general violence or IPV. However, of those respondents who have been the victim of IPV, nearly half (13% out of 27%) have also been the victims of prior non-partner related violence. Similarly, in the case of physical IPV, about half (5% out of 9%) have also been the victim of prior non-partner related violence. In fact, the percentages of Wave One violent offenders and victims and Wave Two IPV victims are nearly identical between Tables 4.4 and 4.5.

Combined, these two tables raise an important question: How often do all three of these phenomena overlap? In other words, how many of the respondents engaged in Wave One offending, were victims of violence at Wave One, and were the victims of IPV at Wave Two? Are the IPV victims and violent offenders displayed in Table 4.4 the same general violence victims and IPV victims displayed in Table 4.5?

In Table 4.6, the frequencies of overlap between violent offending, general violent victimization, and IPV victimization are displayed. As can be seen in this table, a large proportion of this sample (39%) did not engage in any violence and were not victims of any type of violence (general violence or IPV). However, as compared to Tables 4.4 and 4.5, similar proportions of respondents engaged in violence and were the victims of both Wave One general violence and Wave Two IPV. For example, compared to the 13% of respondents who reported violent offenses at Wave One and any type of IPV victimization at Wave Two (Table 4.4) and the 13% of respondents who reported violent victimizations at Wave One and any type of IPV victimization at Wave Two (Table 4.5), 11% of respondents reported all three phenomena (Wave One violent offending and victimization and Wave Two IPV victimization). Taken together, the results from Tables 4.4 through 4.6 are consistent with the expectations of this study: these three phenomena often do co-occur.

Table 4.6. Prevalence of Wave One Violent Offending, General Violent Victimization and Wave Two IPV Victimization

	Percentage of Adolescents Reporting:	
	No W1 Violence or W2 IPV	W1 Offending, W1 Victimization and W2 IPV
Any IPV	39%	11%
Verbal IPV	40%	10%
Physical IPV	48%	04%

N = 6,285

Peer Network Characteristics

The next objective of these analyses is to examine whether and how friendship networks influence IPV victimization. Do the delinquency and violent offending of peer networks influence IPV victimization? Are adolescents with fewer peers more or less likely to become victims of IPV? Is having a higher proportion of opposite sex friends associated with an increase or decrease in IPV victimization? To answer these questions, these analyses examine the effect of peer network delinquency and violent offending, peer network size and density, the centrality of the respondent in his or her network, and the gender composition of the friendship network.

The correlation coefficients between violent offending, violent victimization, IPV victimization, and the peer network characteristics are displayed in Table 4.7. Most of these correlations are statistically significant and go in the expected directions, but all of these correlations are very small based on Cohen's (1988) standard of correlation size. With few exceptions, correlations smaller than 0.50 are considered small.

For example, mean peer network delinquency and violence are both positively and significantly correlated with the respondent's own violent offending and victimization, but these correlations are tiny. Mean peer network delinquency and violence are also positively correlated with IPV victimization, although the correlation between peer network delinquency and IPV victimization is larger compared to peer network violence. The difference between these two correlations is statistically significant[2]. The size of the correlation between peer network delinquency and IPV victimization is about three times as large as the correlation between peer network violence and IPV victimization (the difference between these correlation coefficients is also significant). Overall, however, both of these peer network coefficients have a very weak correlation with IPV victimization.

---

[2] The formula to determine whether these two correlation coefficients were significantly different is as follows: $t = (r_{xy} - r_{zy})* \text{SQRT}[\{(n-3)(1 + r_{xz})\}/ \{2(1 - r_{xy}^2 - r_{xz}^2 - r_{zy}^2 + 2r_{xy}*r_{xz}*r_{zy})\}]$

Table 4.7. Correlation Coefficients—Violent Offending, Violent Victimization, IPV Victimization, and Peer Network Characteristics

	W1 Violent Offending	W1 Violent Victimization	IPV Victim
Mean network delinquency	0.08***	0.06***	0.09***
Mean network violence	0.13***	0.10***	0.03***
Size of peer network	-0.09***	-0.09***	-0.01*
Isolate	0.05***	0.08***	0.01**
In-degree	-0.07***	-0.07***	0.01
Out-degree	-0.12***	0.01***	-0.03***
Density	0.01***	-0.07***	-0.02**
Bonacich centrality	-0.12***	-0.11***	-0.03***
Proportion opposite sex	0.03***	0.03***	0.05***

Displaying Pearson's R Correlations

N = 6,285

* p<.05, ** p<.01, *** p<.001

In light of Kreager's (2004) research on isolation from peer networks and delinquency, the relationship between being an isolate (i.e., having no peers in both the send and receive networks) and the respondent's own violent behavior is surprising. Typically, individuals with few or no peers have lower involvement in deviant behavior. However, in this sample isolates appear to have more involvement with both violent offending and violent victimization. Once again, these correlations are very small.

Consistent with expectations, being an isolate is not strongly associated with IPV victimization. The relationship is positive and significant, but it is also nearly at zero (r = 0.01). Perhaps individuals with few or no friends are less likely to date, and in effect they are less likely to become victims of IPV. However, having a lot of friends is also not strongly or significantly associated with IPV victimization. The overall effect of peer network size is mixed, and often small and insignificant across the three measures of IPV victimization. Having a larger peer network is negatively correlated with the respondent's own violent offending and violent victimization, and very weakly negatively correlated with all three measures of IPV victimization.

Similarly, being nominated as a peer by more individuals is negatively associated with violent offending and violent victimization, and its relationship with IPV victimization is very small and mixed in both direction and significance across all three measures of IPV victimization. The number of other peers nominated by the respondent (the respondent's reach) and the density of the respondent's peer network are only very slightly associated with IPV victimization. The larger the respondent's reach and involvement in denser peer networks, the less likely he or she is to become the victim of IPV.

The centrality of the respondent in his or her peer network is also negatively associated with IPV victimization. Respondents with more central roles in peer networks are less likely to become the victims of IPV. However, the magnitude of this relationship is very small. Overall, it appears that peer network structural characteristics have a very weak relationship with IPV victimization, and the direction of this relationship is not consistent across measures. Some structural characteristics increase the risk of IPV victimization (the size of the peer network, whether the respondent has no peers, the respondent's popularity), while others decreased the risk of IPV victimization (the respondent's reach and centrality in the network and network density).

The gender composition of peer networks is positively associated with Wave One violence and IPV victimization. However, this is the overall effect of gender compositions, and these relationships may vary between males and females. For example, Haynie et al. (2007) found that having more opposite sex friends increased violent offending for females and decreased violent offending for males. Whether peer network gender composition works differently for males and females is examined below.

Gender Differences

Another purpose of these analyses is to compare the experience of IPV victimization between male and female victims. Table 4.8 displays the prevalence of Wave One violence and Wave Two IPV victimization separately for male and female respondents. As expected, a much larger proportion of male respondents have both engaged in violent offending and have been the victims of general violence, and the size of these proportions across violent offending and violent victimization are almost identical. A total of 23% of males in this sample have engaged in violent offending, as compared to 17% of females. Twenty-three percent of males have been the victims of general violence, compared to 16% of females.

Table 4.8. Prevalence of Wave One Violent Offending, General Violent Victimization, and Wave Two IPV Victimization between Adolescent Males and Females

	Male		**Female**
Yes – W1 Violent Offender	23%		17%
No - W1 Violent Offender	21%		39%
Phi Coefficient		0.22**	
Yes – W1 Violent Victim	23%		16%
No - W1 Violent Victim	21%		40%
Phi Coefficient		0.24**	
Yes – W2 IPV Victim, All	13%		15%
No – W2 IPV Victim, All	31%		41%
Phi Coefficient		0.30**	
Yes – W2 IPV Victim, Verbal	12%		14%
No – W2 IPV Victim, Verbal	32%		42%
Phi Coefficient		0.20**	
Yes – W2 IPV Victim, Physical	4%		5%
No – W2 IPV Victim, Physical	40%		51%
Phi Coefficient		0.01*	

N = 6,285
* p<.05, ** p<.01, *** p<.001

Female respondents account for only a slightly larger proportion of IPV victims as compared to male respondents, including the more serious physical violence. A total of 15% of the female respondents reported at least one instance of any type of IPV victimization, and 13% of male respondents reported the same. Fourteen percent of female respondents reported some type of verbal intimidation by an intimate partner, compared to 12% of male respondents. About 5% of female respondents reported physical violence by an intimate partner, compared to 4% of males.

That females and males experience similar rates of verbal intimidation by their intimate partners could be consistent with expectations or contrary to expectations depending on the seriousness of this abuse. That is, males and females should probably have similar rates of less-serious IPV victimization. However, if this verbal abuse is similar to what Stark (2007) calls "coercive control," then females should have higher rates of verbal IPV victimization.

Past research would indicate that females should be much more likely to be the victims of more serious and injurious IPV, including physical violence. However, it is important to keep in mind that Add Health's IPV scale has similar limitations compared to the CTS scale; this scale likely captures a large number of less serious instances of IPV and it does not measure the consequences of this violence. Also, other studies of adolescent IPV that used the Add Health data found similar rates of IPV between males and females (e.g., Halpern et al. 2001). Overall, the difference between these groups is significant, as indicated by the phi coefficient. The size of the phi coefficient for physical IPV victimization is by far the smallest compared to the others (phi = 0.01).

Table 4.9 displays the correlation coefficients between selected peer network variables, Wave One violence, and Wave Two IPV victimization for males and females separately. These peer network measures were selected because they were expected to work differently for males and females, particularly the proportion of opposite sex friends in the peer network.

Almost all of the correlations for both males and females are significant (p-value < 0.001) but again are very small in magnitude. Most do not exceed 0.10. The correlations also do not appear to vary significantly between males and females. The average delinquency and violence in the peer networks works similarly for male and female respondents. Having more delinquent and violent friends is associated with an increase in violent offending, violent victimization, and any type of IPV victimization for both male and female respondents.

Table 4.9. Correlation Coefficients for Peer Network Variables between Male and Female Adolescents

	W1 Violent Offending	W1 Violent Victimization	IPV Victim
	Male Respondents		
Mean network delinquency	0.11***	0.08***	0.08***
Mean network violence	0.11***	0.07***	0.03***
Proportion opposite sex	0.01	0.02**	0.04***
	Female Respondents		
Mean network delinquency	0.07***	0.06***	0.10***
Mean network violence	0.14***	0.12***	0.03***
Proportion opposite sex	0.01*	0.00	0.06***

Displaying Pearson's R Correlations
N = 6,285
* p<.05, ** p<.01, *** p<.001

Fisher's z-test of difference between correlation coefficients was used to determine whether the difference between the correlation coefficients between males and females was significant (Agresti and Finlay 1997).

The z-test is displayed below:

$$r' = (0.5)\log_e \left| \frac{1+r}{1-r} \right| \quad \rightarrow \quad z = \frac{r_1' - r_2'}{\sqrt{\dfrac{1}{n_1 - 3} + \dfrac{1}{n_2 - 3}}}$$

The difference between these correlations for males and females are not significant, with the exception of the correlation between mean peer network violence and any type of IPV victimization ($z = -1.98$, p-value < 0.05). The correlation between mean peer network violence and the respondent's own violent victimization is stronger for females compared to males, but the size of these correlations are small (Pearson's $r = 0.07$ for males and 0.12 for females).

Unexpectedly, the correlation between Wave One violence, IPV victimization, and the proportion of opposite sex friends in the peer network is very small, and does not differ for males and females. The correlations between Wave One violence and the proportion of opposite sex friends are nearly zero for both males and females, and the difference between these correlations between males and females is not significant (p-value < 0.05).

The correlation coefficients between opposite sex friends and all three measures of IPV victimization for both males and females are positive and significant; but, again, they are very small. Also, the difference between these correlations for males and females is not significantly different according to the z-tests (p-value < 0.05).

MULTIVARIATE RESULTS

In Table 4.10 the logistic regression coefficients for the multivariate analyses are displayed. Separate analyses for the three different measures of IPV victimization were conducted (all, verbal, and physical). The results for these analyses were very similar, thus, for space considerations, only the results for the multivariate analyses predicting any type of IPV victimization are displayed.

Table 4.10 is divided into three models. In Model 1, Wave One violent offending is used to predict Wave Two IPV victimization, and in Model 2, Wave One violent victimization is used to predict the same outcome. In Model 3, both Wave One violent offending and violent victimization are used to predict Wave Two IPV victimization.

Table 4.10. Logistic Regression Models Predicting Wave Two IPV Victimization[a]

	Model 1	Model 2	Model 3
	Odds Ratio		
Wave 1 Violent Offending	1.46***	--	1.25*
Wave 1 Violent Victimization	--	1.50***	1.33**
Childhood Maltreatment	1.07	1.06	1.06
Relationship Characteristics			
Relationship Duration	1.01	1.01	1.01
Emotional Intensity	1.01	1.01	1.01
Sexual Activity	1.20***	1.20***	1.20***
Individual Characteristics			
Gender (male)	1.06	1.05	1.02
Age (in years)	1.11**	1.10**	1.11**
African American	1.13	1.12	1.10
Other Race	1.07	1.06	1.06
Unstructured Socializing	1.12*	1.12*	1.12*
Depression	2.14***	2.17***	2.13***
Drug Use	1.36**	1.35**	1.35**
Constant (Std. Error)	-4.02	-3.83	-3.94
	(0.77)	(0.77)	(0.78)
F-Test	11.72***	10.93***	11.02***

* $p<.05$, ** $p<.01$, *** $p<.001$

a. To e space, certain weak and non-significant coefficients are not displayed, including family SES, self-esteem, parental support, hostile school environments, and tobacco use

As shown in Model 1, Wave One violent offending is a significant predictor of Wave Two IPV victimization, even after controlling for several relevant relationship and individual characteristics. Prior involvement in violent offending increases the odds of IPV victimization by 46% (exp[0.38], p-value <0.001). The amount of sexual activity within the relationship is also a salient factor in predicting relationship violence. Increased levels of sexual activity within the relationship increase the odds of IPV victimization by 20% (exp[0.18], p-value < 0.001).

Adolescents who are older and who spend more time in unstructured social activities ("just hanging out") are also significantly more likely to become the victims of IPV. An increase in age increases the odds of IPV victimization by 11% (exp[0.11], p-value < 0.01). Consistent with opportunity theories, unstructured socializing increases the odds of IPV victimization by 12% (exp[0.11], p-value < 0.05). Depression is by far the largest predictor of IPV victimization, more than doubling the odds of IPV victimization (114% or exp[0.76], p-value < 0.001). Drug use increases the odds by 36% (exp[0.31], p-value < 0.01).

As can be seen in Model 2 in Table 4.10, the relationship between Wave One violent victimization (non-partner-related) and Wave Two IPV victimization is nearly identical, net of all of the individual and relationship characteristics. Prior violent victimization is a slightly larger predictor of relationship violence as compared to violent offending, increasing the odds of IPV victimization by 50% (exp[0.41], p-value < 0.001). The size, direction, and significance of sexual activity within the relationship, age, time spent hanging out, depression, and drug use remain virtually unchanged.

Referencing Model 3 in Table 4.10, including both prior violent offending and violent victimization in the model together decreases the size and significance of both effects. Prior violent victimization (not partner-related) is a stronger predictor of relationship violence, increasing the odds of IPV victimization by 33% (exp[0.28], p-value < 0.01). After controlling for prior violent victimization, prior violent offending increases the odds of relationship violence by 25% (exp[0.22], p-value < 0.05). Compared to Model 1, the size of the odds ratio for Wave One violent offending shrank by about 14%. After controlling for Wave One violent offending, the odds ratio for Wave One violent victimization shrank by 11%.

After controlling for both Wave One violent offending and violent victimization, the size of the effect for depression decreased only slightly. Depression remains the strongest predictor of IPV victimization, increasing the odds of IPV victimization by 113% (exp[0.76], p-value < 0.001). Other factors that were significant predictors of Wave Two IPV victimization in Models 1 and 2 remained the same (e.g., time spent hanging out, drug use).

Peer Network Influence

In Table 4.11, the coefficients for an analysis that included peer network characteristics are displayed (Model 2). To allow for a comparison, the coefficients for the analysis not including peer network characteristics are displayed in Model 1. As can be seen here, adding peer network characteristics does not significantly alter the results of this analysis. Prior violent offending increases the odds of Wave Two IPV victimization by 26% (exp[0.23], p-value < 0.05), compared to 25% in Model 1. Wave One violent victimization increases the odds of subsequent IPV victimization by 32% (exp[0.28, p-value <0.01), compared to 33% in Model 1. Additionally, the sexual activity within the relationship, unstructured socializing, the respondent's age, depression, and drug use remain important factors in determining the likelihood of IPV victimization.

Overall, none of the peer network characteristics appears to make a significant difference in the likelihood of IPV victimization. Most of the coefficients are small in size and non-significant. Additionally, similar measures of peer network characteristics have opposite effects on the likelihood of IPV victimization. For example, mean network delinquency decreases the odds of IPV victimization by 3% (exp[-0.03], non-significant). Mean network violence, on the other hand, increases the odds of IPV victimization by 11% (exp[0.10], non-significant).

The size of the peer network and the density of the peer network are associated with a decrease in the odds of IPV victimization, but these coefficients are not significant. Larger peer networks result in a 6% (exp[-0.06], non-significant) decrease in the odds of IPV victimization, and denser peer networks result in a 15% (exp[-0.16], non-significant) decrease in the odds of IPV victimization. Likewise, having no friends (i.e., being an isolate) results in a 1% (exp[0.01], non-significant) increase in the odds of IPV victimization, but is also non-significant.

Table 4.11. Logistic Regression Models Predicting Wave Two IPV Victimization using Peer Network Characteristics[a]

	Model 1	Model 2
	Odds Ratio	
Wave 1 Violent Offending	1.25*	1.26*
Wave 1 Violent Victimization	1.33**	1.32**
Childhood Maltreatment	1.06	1.06
Relationship Characteristics		
Relationship Duration	1.01	1.01
Emotional Intensity	1.01	1.01
Sexual Activity	1.20***	1.20***
Peer Network Characteristics		
Mean Network Delinquency	--	0.97
Mean Network Violence	--	1.11
Size of peer network	--	0.94
Isolate	--	1.01
In-degree	--	1.07
Out-degree	--	1.04
Density	--	0.85
Bonacich centrality	--	1.00
Opposite sex friends	--	1.37
Individual Characteristics		
Gender (male)	1.02	1.03
Age (in years)	1.11**	1.12**
Depression	2.13***	2.13***
Drug Use	1.35**	1.35**
Constant (Std. Error)	-3.94	-4.09
	(0.78)	(0.83)
F-Test	11.02***	7.83***

* $p<.05$, ** $p<.01$, *** $p<.001$

a. To save space, certain weak and insignificant coefficients are not displayed, including family SES, self-esteem, parental support, hostile school environments, and tobacco use.

Although the direction, and not the significance, of the coefficients suggest that more popular students are less likely to become victims of IPV and loner students are slightly more likely to become victims, two other measures of peer network size and popularity (which are also non-significant) show a small association between popularity and an increase in the odds of IPV victimization. The higher the number of others who nominate the respondent as a peer (in-degree) and the higher the number of others who are nominated by the respondent as peers are both associated with an increase in the odds of IPV victimization (7% and 4%, respectively, but not significant). The centrality of the respondent in his or her network has virtually no effect on the odds of IPV victimization (0%, or exp[-0.00], non-significant). Overall, however, none of these coefficients are significant.

The proportion of opposite sex friends in the respondent's peer network has the largest non-significant effect compared to all of the other peer network characteristics. Having more opposite sex friends is associated with a 37% (exp[0.31], non-significant) increase in the odds of IPV victimization. However, this measure may work differently for males and females, and this possibility is explored later in this chapter.

In addition to using all of the peer network measures in one analysis, each of these measures was also analyzed individually in this same analysis. The results remained the same. Interaction terms between each of the peer network characteristics and the other measures used in this analyses (including prior violence, relationship characteristics and individual characteristics) were also added, and each of these interaction terms produced only small and non-significant effects. Overall, the peer network characteristics do not strongly or significantly influence the odds of IPV victimization.

Gender Differences

As can be seen in the above analyses, gender does not have a strong or significant effect on the odds of IPV victimization. However, there is evidence that males and females have different experiences with violent offending, general violent victimization, and IPV victimization. Thus, special attention was given to the role of gender in these analyses.

Table 4.12. Logistic Regression Models Predicting Wave Two IPV Victimization Separately for Adolescent Males and Females[a]

	Males	Females	Z-Test
	Odds Ratio		
Wave 1 Violent Offending	1.54**	1.03	1.92*
Wave 1 Violent Victimization	1.21	1.52***	-1.13
Childhood Maltreatment	1.16*	0.97	2.31**
Relationship Characteristics			
Relationship Duration	0.99	1.03	-0.58
Emotional Intensity	1.02	1.02	-0.01
Sexual Activity	1.18**	1.19***	-0.80
Individual Characteristics			
Age (in years)	1.16**	1.10*	0.80
African American	1.33	0.99	1.26
Other Race	1.11	1.00	0.44
School Trouble	1.14	0.87	2.26**
Parental Supervision	1.05	0.97	0.75
Unstructured Socializing	1.06	1.16*	-0.86
Depression	2.07***	2.21***	-0.27
Smoking	1.00	1.01*	-1.38
Drug Use	1.36*	1.31	0.18
Constant (Std. Error)	-5.66	-3.83	
	(1.15)	(0.77)	
F-Test	6.94***	7.48***	

* p<.05, ** p<.01, *** p<.001

a. To save space, certain weak and non-significant coefficients are not displayed, including family SES, self-esteem, parental support, hostile school environments, and tobacco use

Several interactions were attempted in order to determine whether gender moderates any of these relationships. These interactions included gender and prior violent offending, gender and prior victimization (both general violent victimization and parental maltreatment), gender and relationship characteristics (particularly duration), and gender and depression. The only two interaction terms that were significant were the interactions between gender and parental maltreatment (exp[0.18] = 1.20, p-value < 0.05) and gender and school trouble (exp[0.21] = 1.24, p-value < 0.05).

With some evidence of gender differences, the same analyses as above were applied to males and females separately. The results of these analyses are displayed in Table 4.12. To determine whether there are significant differences between males and females, a z-test for differences between two regression coefficients was conducted (see Paternoster et al. 1998 and Clogg et al. 1995). This test essentially determines whether two regression coefficients estimated within two groups are significantly different (Paternoster et al. 1998). The formula for this test is displayed below:

$$Z = \frac{b_1 - b_2}{\sqrt{SEb_1{}^2 + SEb_2{}^2}}$$

The z-values for the differences between these coefficients are displayed in the far right column in Table 4.12. As can be seen in this table, there are few significant differences in effects between males and females.

Consistent with the interaction terms applied to the entire sample, significant differences in coefficients are limited to parental maltreatment (z = 2.31, p-value < 0.01), and school trouble (z = 2.26, p-value < 0.01). The experience of childhood abuse by parents or guardians increases the odds of IPV victimization by 16% (exp[0.15], p-value < 0.05) for males, while it decreases the odds of IPV victimization by 3% (exp[-0.03], non-significant) for females. An increase in the amount of trouble getting along with others in school results in a 14% (exp[0.13], non-significant) increase in the odds of IPV victimization for males and a 13% (exp[-0.14], non-significant) decrease in odds for females.[3]

Even though the interaction term between gender and Wave One violent offending was not significant (exp[0.34] = 1.40, non-

---

[3] Because they were small and non-significant in the analyses for males and females separately, the coefficients for school trouble for males and females were not included in Table 4.12.

significant), the difference in coefficients for males and females for this measure is significant ($z = 1.92$, p-value < 0.05). Prior violent offending is associated with a larger increase in the odds for males ($\exp[0.43] = 1.54$, p-value < 0.01) than for females ($\exp[0.03] = 1.03$, non-significant).

As can be seen in this table, all of the other measures have similar effects on males and females, in terms of size, direction, and significance. Depression is the strongest predictor of IPV victimization for both males and females, increasing the odds of IPV victimization by 107% ($\exp[0.73]$, p-value < 0.001) for males and 121% ($\exp[0.79]$, p-value < 0.001) for females. The amount of sexual activity within the relationship also significantly increases the odds of IPV victimization for both males and females (18% and 19%, respectively). The difference between these coefficients for males and females is not significant.

Although the difference between these coefficients is not significant for this measure, Wave One violent victimization appears to have a stronger and significant influence on Wave Two IPV victimization for females as compared to males. Wave One violent victimization increases the odds of Wave Two IPV victimization by 52% ($\exp[0.42]$, p-value < 0.01), and only 22% ($\exp[0.19]$, p-value > 0.05) for males. Thus, it appears that violent males are more likely to end up in troublesome and abusive relationships, while victimized females are more prone to end up in these troubled relationships.

Interaction terms between gender and peer network characteristics were also attempted in earlier analyses. None of these interactions were significant. Separate analyses were done for males and females which included these peer network characteristics, and, again, no significant differences were found in how peer network characteristics influence the risk of IPV victimization for males and females. In fact, within groups (for males and females), peer network characteristics did not significantly influence the risk of IPV victimization.

Table 4.13. Logistic Regression Models Predicting Wave Two IPV Victimization Separately for Adolescent Males and Females with Peer Network Characteristics[a]

	Males	Females	Z-Test
	Odds Ratio		
Wave 1 Violent Offending	1.55**	1.05	1.92*
Wave 1 Violent Victimization	1.20	1.49**	-1.13
Childhood Maltreatment	1.16*	0.98	2.31**
Relationship Characteristics			
Relationship Duration	0.99	1.03	-0.58
Emotional Intensity	1.01	1.01	-0.01
Sexual Activity	1.19**	1.19***	-0.80
Peer Network Characteristics			
Mean Network Delinquency	0.95	1.00	-0.34
Mean Network Violence	1.11	1.06	0.29
Size of peer network	0.97	0.91	-0.21
Isolate	0.96	1.09	-0.45
In-degree	1.04	1.09	0.05
Out-degree	1.05	1.04	0.45
Density	1.40	0.53	0.96
Bonacich centrality	0.89	1.09	-0.64
Opposite sex friends	1.21	1.53	-0.48
Constant (Std. Error)	-6.07	-3.07	
	(1.25)	(1.12)	
F-Test	4.63***	5.54***	

* $p<.05$, ** $p<.01$, *** $p<.001$

a. To save space, certain weak and insignificant coefficients are not displayed including age, race, depression, tobacco use, drug use, school trouble, physical development, family SES, and self-esteem.

The results of these analyses are displayed in Table 4.13. In the far right column, the z-test of difference between coefficients is displayed. These analyses were particularly concerned with peer network delinquency and violence and the proportion of opposite sex friends in the respondent's network. Just as what was observed in the previous analysis that included peer network characteristics (Table 4.11), adding peer network measures does not alter the size, direction, or significance of the other coefficients.

Although the peer network characteristics do not appear to be salient factors in determining IPV victimization and these coefficients are not significantly different for males and females, there are some trivial differences in the direction and magnitude of these measures between males and females. Peer delinquency decrease the odds of IPV victimization for males by 5% (exp[-0.05], non-significant), while it has almost no effect on female IPV victimization (exp[0.00], non-significant). Another small difference between males and females is the proportion of opposite sex friends. Having more opposite sex friends increases the odds of IPV victimization for both males and females, although the effect of this measure is larger for females. Having more opposite sex friends increases the odds of IPV victimization by 53% (exp[0.42], non-significant) for females and 21% (exp[0.19], non-significant) for males. Although these coefficients are not significant, the magnitude and direction of this coefficient for females is consistent with expectations. Having more male friends (who, on average, are more violent and less nurturing) increases the odds of IPV victimization. However, that the proportion of opposite sex friends does not decrease the risk of IPV victimization for males is not consistent with expectations.

Popularity appears to work differently for males and females, but, again, these differences are not significant nor are the coefficients for these measures within groups. Being an isolate decreases the odds of IPV victimization for males (odds ratio = 0.96, non-significant), while it increases the odds of victimization for females (odds ratio = 1.09, non-significant). The size of the peer network decreases the odds of IPV victimization for both males and females (3% and 9%, respectively; having more friends decreases the odds of being in an abusive relationship. However, the amount of sent and received peer nominations increases the odds of IPV victimization.

Although the difference for this measure between males and females is not significant, density appears to have a different effect on IPV victimization for males and females. Having a denser peer network is associated with a large increase in the odds of IPV victimization for males (40%, exp[0.34], non-significant) and an even larger decrease in the odds of victimization for females (-47%, exp[-0.64], non-significant). Again, each of these coefficients and the difference in these coefficients for males and females is non-significant. Overall, peer network characteristics did not have a meaningful impact on the risk of IPV victimization for males and females, and the differences between these two groups were not meaningful either.

CONCLUSIONS

The results of these analyses indicate that the overlap between victims and offenders that applies to general violent behavior also applies to IPV victimization. Prior violence and IPV victimization are associated with one another, which is especially evident in the multivariate analyses and not the bivariate analyses. Also, a large proportion of IPV victims (about half) report past involvement in violent offending and violent victimization.

In the multivariate analyses, both prior violent offending and violent victimization are predictive of IPV victimization, even after controlling for several relevant factors. Prior violent victimization is a slightly stronger risk factor for IPV victimization as compared to violent offending. Just as past violent victimization is predictive of future violent victimization, past violent victimization is also predictive of this particular type of victimization.

These analyses were also focused on the influence of peer networks and possible differences between males and females. However, peer network characteristics did not significantly influence the risk of IPV victimization, nor did these characteristics moderate the effects of any of the other variables. Both peer delinquency and violence had only small relationships with IPV victimization, and these relationships were not significant. Measures representing the size of peer networks and the popularity of the respondents also did not have a large influence on the risk of IPV victimization and were non-significant. Both popular students and "loners" appear to be at similar risk for IPV victimization.

The fact that males and females did not vary significantly in their risk of IPV victimization is surprising. Research on both adolescent and adult IPV suggests that males and females probably experience similar rates of IPV victimization, although females are more likely to be the victims of serious violence. In the present analyses, even for more serious physical IPV victimization, males and females had similar rates of victimization. However, the questions used in the Add Health survey to measure IPV victimization likely capture many non-serious instances of IPV victimization. This series of questions includes only two physical items, and these items could range from non-serious to very serious. Perhaps if more questions were used to ask about more serious forms of physical assault and injury, more differences between males and females would have emerged.

In terms of the separate analyses of males and females, one of the only significant differences between males and females was that past violent offending was a larger and significant predictor of IPV victimization for males compared to females. This finding may reflect the fact that mutual IPV victimization is just as common if not more common among males as compared to females, while females are more likely to be the victims of one-sided violence. In other words, violent males may be more likely to end up in relationships with violent females, while victimized females are more likely to end up in relationships with abusive males. However, this explanation is speculative, and whether males and females differ in rates of mutual and one-sided couple violence is further explored in Chapter 6.

The results of these analyses did not provide much support for social learning theories. The lack of relationship between peer network delinquency and IPV victimization is contrary to the expectations of both opportunity theories and social learning theories. According to lifestyle exposure theory, attachment to delinquent peers should increase the risk of IPV victimization because of the exposure to risk and because adolescents likely choose abusive partners from deviant peer networks. However, the results of these analyses do not support this notion. Also, social learning theories hold that attachment to deviant peer networks should increase one's own deviance.

However, that prior violent offending, prior violent victimization, and unstructured socializing were predictive of IPV victimization provides support for lifestyle exposure theory. Prior violence (offending and victimization) represent exposure to risk, and this exposure is associated with an increase in the odds of IPV victimization. Unstructured socializing provides opportunity for adolescents to become involved with abusive partners. Also, during unstructured socializing, responsible adults are not present to recognize abusive behaviors and intervene when abuse occurs.

Overall, the results of these analyses indicate that IPV shares some commonalities with general violence. This finding would support the "violence perspective" favored by Felson (2006; Felson and Lane 2010). However, these analyses examined all instances of IPV. There are likely multiple types of IPV in these data (e.g., intimate terrorism, situational couple violence), and these conclusions may not apply to all of these types. Additional analyses are conducted in Chapter 6 to examine whether different types of IPV have different risk factors.

Now that the risk factors of IPV victimization have been examined, the next Chapter of results examines deviant behaviors associated with IPV victimization. The next set of analyses examines whether Wave Two IPV victimization is associated with Wave Two violent offending, general delinquency, and drug use, net of past occurrences of these behaviors.

CHAPTER 5

Behaviors Associated with Adolescent Intimate Partner Violence Victimization

INTRODUCTION

In this chapter, behaviors associated with IPV victimization are examined in three ways. First, there is an analysis of whether Wave Two violent offending, violent victimization, general delinquency, and drug use are associated with Wave Two IPV victimization. Several studies have established a link between IPV victimization and a number of deviant behaviors. However, many of these studies failed to take into account prior deviant behavior. As observed in Chapter 4, past deviant behaviors increase the odds of IPV victimization. Given that past deviant behaviors are highly predictive of future deviant behaviors, and deviant behaviors are associated with an increase in the odds of IPV victimization, the link between IPV and within-wave offending may be spurious[4].

Second, these analyses examine whether and how certain peer network characteristics influence these relationships. These analyses are particularly interested in the link between peer network delinquency and violence. According to Agnew's General Strain Theory, involvement in deviant peer networks may moderate the link between

---

[4] Ideally, this study would examine the relationship between Wave One IPV victimization and Wave Two Deviant behaviors. However, the Add Health data do not include a Wave One measure of IPV victimization.

111

IPV victimization and offending. In other words, given that deviant peer networks influence individual offending, involvement in a deviant peer network may increase the likelihood that adolescent victims of IPV will respond to this victimization with deviant behavior (violent offending, general delinquency, or drug use).

The third way in which these analyses examine the link between IPV victimization and deviant behavior is by examining possible gender differences in offending behaviors linked to IPV victimization. In other words, is IPV victimization for males compared to females differentially associated with violent offending? Is IPV victimization more or less associated with drug use for females as compared to males? Also, are there differences in how certain peer network characteristics influence or moderate the relationship between IPV victimization and offending behaviors for males and females? Specifically, does having more opposite sex friends moderate the relationship between IPV victimization and offending behaviors? Research indicates that having a high proportion of opposite sex friends increases violent offending for females and decreases violent offending for males.

The analyses and results presented in this chapter are divided into three main sections. First, this chapter provides a description of the sample and measures used in these analyses. Second, the bivariate relationships between IPV victimization and violent offending, general delinquency, and drug use are presented and discussed. In the final section of this chapter, the multivariate results are presented and discussed. In this last section, Wave Two IPV victimization is used to predict Wave Two violent offending, general delinquency, and drug use.

THE SAMPLE AND DESCRIPTIVE STATISTICS

The data used in this chapter of results are the same data used in Chapter 4. The respondents analyzed in this chapter met the following criteria: (a) they were included in the first three waves of interviews; (b) they were involved in at least one romantic or non-romantic relationship during the second wave interview; and, (c) they were between the ages of 11 and 18 at the time of the second interview.

Table 5.1. Descriptive Statistics for Dependent Measures—Violent Offending, Violent Victimization, General Delinquency, and Drug Use

Variable	Mean/Percent	Std Dev	Range
Violent Offending			
Wave One Violent Offending	0.68	1.01	0 - 5
Wave Two Violent Offending	0.44	0.91	0 - 5
Violent Victimization			
Wave One Violent Victimization	0.44	0.91	0 - 4
Wave Two Violent Victimization	0.26	0.67	0 - 4
General Delinquency			
Wave One Delinquency	1.27	1.79	0 - 9
Wave Two Delinquency	0.98	1.60	0 - 9
Drug Use			
Wave One Drug Use	19%	--	--
Wave Two Drug Use	21%	--	--

N = 6,279

Because this chapter uses the same data and many of the same measures as Chapter 4, the descriptive statistics for most of these measures are the same as those displayed in Tables 4.1 and 4.2. The IPV and violent offending measures described in Table 4.1 are the same ones used in these analyses, although the count version of IPV is used as an independent measure in the following analyses. Wave Two violent offending, violent victimization, general delinquency, and drug use are the dependent measures.

The Wave Two dependent variables and their Wave One counterparts are described in Table 5.1. As can be seen in this table, respondents had a higher average of violent offending and violent victimization in Wave One as compared to Wave Two. Respondents engaged in an average of 0.68 out of a possible 5 violent offenses in Wave One, and an average of 0.44 offenses in Wave Two. Respondents were victimized by an average of 0.44 violent offenses in Wave One, and 0.26 in Wave Two. Involvement in general delinquency also declined in Wave Two compared to Wave One. Respondents committed an average of 1.27 out of a possible 9 delinquent acts in Wave One, compared to 0.98 in Wave Two. As described in the previous chapter of results, the decline in violent offending, violent victimization, and delinquency is likely due to telescoping.

Unlike violence and delinquency, drug use increased slightly in Wave Two. A total of 19% of the respondents reported using at least one type of drug in Wave One (including marijuana, cocaine, hallucinogens, and intravenous drugs), whereas 21% reported drug use in Wave Two. This increase in drug use is likely due to the fact that older adolescents have higher rates of drug use. According to the Monitoring the Future study, high school seniors tend to have higher rates of marijuana use and use of other illicit drugs compared to classmates in lower grades (Johnston et al. 2009).

BIVARIATE RESULTS: THE PREVALENCE OF WAVE TWO IPV VICTIMIZATION, VIOLENT OFFENDING, VIOLENT VICTIMIZATION, DELINQUENCY, AND DRUG USE

Displayed in Table 5.2 are the correlation coefficients between three measures of Wave Two IPV victimization (all abuse, verbal abuse, physical abuse) and four Wave Two deviant behaviors (violent offending, violent victimization, delinquency, drug use). As can be seen in this table, all four of these Wave Two deviant behaviors are positively and significantly correlated with all three measures of Wave Two IPV victimization. However, the magnitudes of all of these correlations are very small. None of these correlations exceed 0.14, and correlations below 0.50 are generally considered to be weak (Cohen 1988). All of these correlations are weak, but physical IPV victimization has the weakest correlation with each type of behavior. The size of the correlation between physical IPV victimization and drug use is half the size of the same correlation for all types of abuse and verbal abuse (Pearson's $r = 0.12$ and 0.06, respectively), and the difference in size between these correlations is significant.

Table 5.3 describes the prevalence of violent offending, violent victimization, general delinquency, and drug use across three measures of IPV victimization and the first two waves of data. These frequencies represent how often these four behaviors overlapped with Wave Two IPV victimization, and the purpose of these tables is to observe how often these phenomena co-occur. At the top of Table 5.3 we observe that only a small fraction of the overall sample engaged in both violent offending at Wave Two and were the victims of IPV victimization at Wave Two. This is particularly true for the overlap between offending and physical IPV victimization. Only 2% of the sample were physically assaulted by their intimate partners and engaged in violent offending at Wave Two. Only 1% of the overall sample engaged in violent offending over both waves of data and were the victims of physical IPV. The overlap between any type of IPV victimization and Wave One violent offending is much larger, at 13%. Three percent of the sample were victims of any type of IPV at Wave Two and engaged in violent offending over both waves of data.

Table 5.2. Correlation Coefficients – Wave Two IPV Victimization, and Wave Two Violent Offending, Violent Victimization, General Delinquency, and Drug Use

IPV Victimization	Violent Offending	Violent Victimization	Delinquency	Drug Use
Any Abuse	0.11***	0.11***	0.14***	0.12***
Verbal Abuse	0.10***	0.10***	0.14***	0.12***
Physical Abuse	0.09***	0.09***	0.10***	0.06***

Displaying Pearson's r Correlations
N = 6,279
*p<0.05, **p<.01, ***p<.001

Below violent offending in Table 5.3, the frequencies of Wave One and Wave Two violent victimization across three measures of Wave Two IPV victimization are displayed. The overlap between IPV victimization and violent victimization is almost identical to that of violent offending. Thirteen percent of the overall sample were victims of general violence in Wave One and victimized by an intimate partner in Wave Two. Only a very small proportion of the sample were both victims of any form of IPV and victims of general violence during both waves of data (5%).

According to the frequencies in overlap for general delinquency and IPV victimization displayed in Table 5.3, a larger proportion of the sample engaged in delinquent acts and were victimized by their intimate partners. Seventeen percent of the sample both engaged in delinquency at Wave One and were victimized by intimate partners at

Wave Two, and 14% reported delinquent acts at the Wave Two interview and were victims of IPV. A total of 11% of the overall sample reported delinquent acts during both waves of data and were victimized by intimate partners. Similar proportions of respondents were victims of verbal IPV and engaged in delinquency compared to any type of IPV victimization. Given the lower prevalence of physical IPV victimization, a much lower proportion of the sample reported both IPV victimization delinquency at both waves (4%).

Table 5.3. Prevalence of Wave One and Wave Two Violent Offending, Violent Victimization, General Delinquency, and Drug Use Across Three Measures of IPV Victimization

	Percentage of Adolescents Reporting:		
	Violent Offending		
	Wave One	Wave Two	Both Waves
W2 IPV	13%	5%	3%
W2 IPV – Verbal	12%	4%	3%
W2 IPV – Physical	5%	2%	1%
	Violent Victimization		
	Wave One	Wave Two	Both Waves
W2 IPV	13%	7%	5%
W2 IPV – Verbal	12%	6%	5%
W2 IPV – Physical	5%	3%	2%
	General Delinquency		
	Wave One	Wave Two	Both Waves
W2 IPV	17%	14%	11%
W2 IPV – Verbal	16%	13%	11%
W2 IPV – Physical	6%	5%	4%
	Drug Use		
	Wave One	Wave Two	Both Waves
W2 IPV	8%	8%	4%
W2 IPV – Verbal	7%	7%	4%
W2 IPV – Physical	3%	3%	1%

N = 6,279

At the bottom of Table 5.3 frequencies of drug use and IPV victimization are displayed across Waves One and Two. Compared to violent offending and delinquency, drug use and IPV do not co-occur as often. Only 8% of the sample used drugs at Wave One and were victimized by intimate partners at Wave Two. The same proportion, 8%, engaged in drug use at Wave Two and were IPV victims. Only 4% of the sample were IPV victims at Wave Two and reported drug use at both interviews. Overall, based on this table it appears that delinquency and IPV victimization co-occur most often.

Peer Network Characteristics

In the last chapter of results we found that in bivariate analyses, peer network delinquency and violence were both positively and significantly associated with IPV victimization, although the strength of this association was not large. In the multivariate analyses in Chapter 4, the coefficients for all of the peer network characteristics were very small and non-significant. In this chapter of results, peer network delinquency and violence are controlled for in the analyses predicting violent offending, violent victimization, delinquency, and drug use. Also, we examine whether these network characteristics moderate the relationship between IPV victimization and these deviant behaviors.

Consistent with past research on peer delinquency and individual delinquency (e.g., Haynie 2002), these data show that mean peer network delinquency and violence positively influence the respondent's own deviant behavior. However, just as we have observed with all of the previous correlations, these correlations are very weak. Based on the correlation coefficients displayed in Table 5.4, mean network delinquency has a weak positive association with violent offending, violent victimization, and delinquency. Given that many other researchers have found that peer delinquency and individual offending are strongly correlated, these correlations are surprisingly low (all are 0.08 or lower). However, the mean peer network delinquency measure captures only minor delinquency (e.g., smoking, truancy), whereas the respondent's measure of delinquency captures both minor and serious (e.g., motor vehicle theft, burglary) forms of delinquency. Mean peer network delinquency has the strongest correlation with drug use (Pearson's $r = 0.18$).

Table 5.4. Correlation Coefficients – Wave Two Violent Offending, General Delinquency, Drug Use, and Peer Network Delinquency and Violence

Peer Network Measures	Violent Offending	Violent Victim	Delinquency	Drug Use
Delinquency	0.06***	0.06***	0.08***	0.18***
Violence	0.09***	0.12***	0.09***	0.05***

Displaying Pearson's r Correlations
N = 6,279
*p<0.05, **p<.01, ***p<.001

Mean peer network violence is also positively associated with violent offending, violent victimization, delinquency, and drug use. Just as we observed with mean peer network delinquency, the correlations between mean peer network violence and all of these measures of deviance is very weak (Pearson's r < 0.13 for all four deviant behaviors).

Gender Differences
Another objective of these analyses is to examine whether the association between deviant behaviors and IPV victimization varies between males and females. The proportions in Table 5.5 represent how often the outcome measures overlap with IPV victimization across both waves of data for males and females.

Referencing the top half of Table 5.5, we observe that, compared to females, a much larger proportion of male respondents engaged in violent offending and were victims of general violence at Wave One and reported IPV victimization at Wave Two (18% compared to 10%, for both violent offending and violent victimization). Similar proportions of males and females reported IPV victimization at Wave Two and engaged in violent offending during the same wave (6% of males, 4% of females). A larger proportion of males were victims of general violence and IPV at wave two compared to females (11% compared to 4%). Only a small proportion of males (4%) engaged in violent offending at both waves of data and were victims of IPV, and an even smaller percentage of females (2%) reported the same. Nine percent of males and only 3% of females were victims of general violence during both waves and were victimized by their romantic partners.

Table 5.5. Prevalence of Wave One and Wave Two Violent Offending, Violent Victimization, General Delinquency, and Drug Use Across IPV Victimization for Males and Females Separately

	Percentage of Adolescents Reporting:		
	Violent Offending		
W2 IPV Victim	Wave One	Wave Two	Both Waves
Males	18%	6%	4%
Females	10%	4%	2%
	Violent Victimization		
W2 IPV Victim	Wave One	Wave Two	Both Waves
Males	18%	11%	9%
Females	10%	4%	3%
	General Delinquency		
W2 IPV Victim	Wave One	Wave Two	Both Waves
Males	20%	16%	14%
Females	15%	12%	9%
	Drug Use		
W2 IPV Victim	Wave One	Wave Two	Both Waves
Males	8%	9%	4%
Females	7%	7%	4%

N = 6,279

Based on the frequencies for the overlap between IPV victimization and delinquency displayed in Table 5.5., the overlap between these two phenomena is again larger for men compared to women. A larger proportion of men reported both delinquent acts and IPV victimization. Fourteen percent of the males reported delinquent acts during both waves of data and IPV victimization at Wave Two, compared to only 9% of females.

According to the frequencies of drug use and IPV victimization displayed at the bottom of Table 5.5, it appears that similar proportions of males and females reported both drug use and IPV victimization. In fact, the same proportion of males and females (4%) reported drug use at both waves of data and IPV victimization at Wave Two. Thus, the association between drug use and IPV victimization may not vary greatly between males and females.

In Table 5.6, the correlations between peer network characteristics (mean network delinquency and violence and the proportion of opposite sex friends in the network) and the outcome measures (violent offending, violent victimization, delinquency, and drug use) are presented for males and females. For both males and females, mean peer network delinquency and violence are both positively and significantly associated with the outcome measures, but these associations are very weak. There are some significant differences in the sizes of these correlation coefficients for males and females. The difference in the correlation coefficients between mean network delinquency and Wave Two violent offending for males and females is significant ($z = 4.42$, p-value < 0.001). This relationship is stronger for males ($r = 0.09$) than for females ($r = 0.04$), but this relationship is still weak for both groups. The association between peer network delinquency and Wave Two delinquency is stronger for females ($r = 0.10$) compared to males ($r = 0.07$; $z = -2.66$, p-value < 0.01), as is the relationship between peer network violence and Wave Two drug use (female $r = 0.07$, male $r = 0.04$; $z = -2.65$, p-value < 0.01). Again, however, all of these correlations are weak.

The correlation between the proportion of opposite sex friends and the outcome measures is very weak. The proportion of opposite sex friends is positively and significantly associated with violent offending for males, but the size of this coefficient is very small (Pearson's $r = 0.02$). However, the difference in the size of this coefficient between males and females is significant (female Pearson's $r = -0.01$, p-value > 0.05; $z = 2.64$, p-value < 0.01). The proportion of opposite sex friends is negatively associated with all three outcome measures for females, which is not consistent with expectations. However, again, these correlations are very small and not significant. Based on these bivariate relationships, it appears that having opposite sex friendships is not associated with any type of offending for males and females.

Table 5.6. Correlation Coefficients for Peer Network Characteristics and Violent Offending, General Delinquency, and Drug Use across Males and Females

	W2 Violent Off.	W2 Violent Vict.	W2 Delinquency	W2 Drug Use
Peer Network:	**Males**			
Delinquency	0.09***	0.06***	0.07***	0.17***
Violence	0.08***	0.06***	0.07***	0.04***
Opp. Sex Friends	0.02**	0.01	-0.02*	0.01
Peer Network:	**Females**			
Delinquency	0.04***	0.05***	0.10***	0.18***
Violence	0.09***	0.08***	0.09***	0.07***
Opp. Sex Friends	-0.01	0.02*	-0.01	-0.02*

Displaying Pearson's r Correlations

N = 6,279

*p<0.05, **p<.01, ***p<.001

MULTIVARIATE RESULTS

In Table 5.7 coefficients predicting Wave Two violent offending using negative binomial regression are displayed. Each model contains the unstandardized coefficient (left) and the incident rate ratio (right). The incident rate ratio (IRR) reflects the percent of change in the expected count of the outcome, which in this table is violent offending. Referencing Model 1, Wave Two IPV victimization is positively and significantly associated with violent offending. A one-unit increase in IPV victimization is associated with a 12% increase in the expected count of Wave Two violent offending (exp[0.11], p-value < 0.001). Childhood abuse by parents is also associated with violent offending, increasing the expected count of violent offending by 13% (exp[0.12], p-value < 0.001).

Gender has a strong relationship with violent offending. Males have a rate of violent offending that is 2.73 times higher than females (exp[1.00], p-value < 0.001). In addition to gender, race (being African American or from another non-white race or ethnicity), having trouble getting along with others in school, depression, drunkenness, and drug use are also positively associated with violent offending. Older adolescents and adolescents from wealthier homes, in contrast, engage in less offending.

In the second model in Table 5.7, both Wave One violent offending and Wave One victimization have been controlled for. As expected, these items are strongly associated with Wave Two violent offending and adding these items reduces the size of the Wave Two IPV victimization coefficient. However, the effect of IPV victimization does not shrink substantially. The incident rate ratio is reduced to 1.09 (exp[0.08], p-value < 0.01) from 1.12 in Model 1 (exp[0.08], p-value < 0.01). The effect of parental maltreatment is also not reduced substantially; the incident rate ratio goes from 1.13 in Model 1 to 1.10 in Model 2 (exp[0.10], p-value < 0.001).

The other coefficients maintain roughly the same size, direction and significance after controlling for prior violence in Model 2, with the exception of gender and school trouble. The incident rate ratio for gender is reduced in size from 2.73 in Model 1 to 1.87 in Model 2 (exp[0.59], p-value < 0.001). School trouble also shrinks in size and becomes insignificant (exp[0.02] = 1.02, p-value > 0.05). Being African American, depressed, an excessive drinker and drug user are all associated with an increase in violent offending, while age and social class are still associated with a decrease in violent offending.

In Model 3 an interaction term is added between Wave One violent offending and Wave Two IPV victimization. At all levels of IPV victimization, high Wave One violent offending is associated with more Wave Two violent offending. We might have expected that IPV victimization would exacerbate the effect of prior violent offending, causing a sharp increase in Wave Two violent offending for individuals with the highest levels of prior violent offending. However, that was not the case in these analyses. The significant interaction term indicates that individuals with the lowest levels of Wave One violent offending experience the sharpest rise in Wave Two violent offending for every one-unit increase in IPV victimization, as compared to individuals with the highest levels of Wave One violent offending who experience a smaller rate of increase in Wave Two violent offending for every one-unit increase in Wave Two IPV victimization. A graph of this interaction is displayed in Figure 5.1.

Table 5.7. Negative Binomial Models Predicting Wave Two Violent Offending[a]

	Model 1	Model 2	Model 3
		IR Ratio	
Wave Two IPV Victimization	1.12***	1.09**	1.17***
Childhood Maltreatment	1.13***	1.10***	1.10***
Wave One Violent Offending	--	1.35***	1.40***
Wave One Violent Victimization	--	1.45***	1.44***
Wave One Violent Offending*	--	--	0.95*
Wave Two IPV Victimization			
Individual Characteristics			
Gender (male)	2.73***	1.87***	1.88***
Age (in years)	0.84***	0.85***	0.86***
African American	1.70***	1.36**	1.36**
Other Race	1.34***	1.10	1.11
School Trouble	1.17***	1.02	1.02
Family SES	0.89***	0.91***	0.91***
Unstructured Socializing	1.02	1.04	1.04
Depression	1.60***	1.41***	1.41***
Self-Esteem	1.10	1.03	1.04
Drunkenness	1.20***	1.16***	1.16***
Drug Use	1.54***	1.35***	1.33***
Constant (Std. Error)	-0.24***	-0.17***	-0.27***
	(0.56)	(0.56)	(0.07)
F-Test	59.92***	60.12***	61.14***

* $p<.05$, ** $p<.01$, *** $p<.001$

a. To e space, certain weak and non-significant coefficients are not displayed, including relationship characteristics, physical development, parental supervision, tobacco use, and two-parent home.

Figure 5.1: Interaction between Wave One Violent Offending and Wave Two IPV Victimization

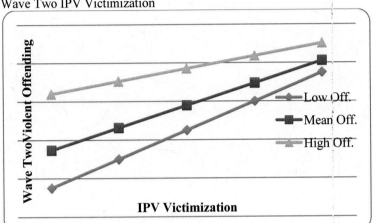

In Table 5.8 Wave Two IPV victimization is used to predict Wave Two general violent victimization (i.e., non-partner related victimization). In Model 1, both IPV victimization and childhood maltreatment have a moderately strong relationship with Wave Two violent victimization. Both of these measures of victimization are associated with an increase in the expected count of subsequent violent victimization ((IPV victimization: exp[0.13] = 1.13, p-value < 0.001); (childhood maltreatment: exp[0.14] = 1.15, p-value < 0.01)).

Unlike the models predicting Wave Two violent offending, the amount of sexual activity within the relationship is significantly associated with an increase in the expected count of violent victimization. A one-unit increase in the amount of sexual activity within the relationship increases the expected count of non-partner related Wave Two violent victimization 9%, holding all other variables constant (exp[0.09], p-value < 0.01). Also, unlike the models predicting violent offending age is not significantly associated with violent victimization (exp[-0.03] = 0.97, p-value > 0.05).

Consistent with what was observed in the models predicting Wave Two violent offending, gender (being male), race, depression, excessive drinking, and drug use are all positively and significantly correlated with Wave Two violent victimization. The relationship between gender and violent victimization is quite strong; the expected count of violent victimization for males is 3.75 times greater compared to females (exp[1.32], p-value < 0.001). In addition to these relationships, physical development and the amount of trouble these adolescent have getting along with others in school (school trouble) are also associated with an increase in victimization.

Table 5.8. Negative Binomial Models Predicting Wave Two Violent Victimization[a]

	Model 1	Model 2	Model 3
		IR Ratio	
Wave Two IPV Victimization	1.13***	1.10*	1.21***
Childhood Maltreatment	1.15***	1.12**	1.11**
Wave One Violent Victimization	--	1.88***	1.97***
Wave One Violent Offending	--	1.10*	1.10*
Wave One Violent Victim*	--	--	0.92*
Wave Two IPV Victimization			
Relationship Characteristics			
Sexual Activity	1.09**	1.07*	1.07*
Individual Characteristics			
Gender (male)	3.75***	2.49***	2.49***
Age (in years)	0.97	0.98	0.98
African American	1.72***	1.43**	1.43**
Other Race	1.60***	1.34*	1.34*
Physical Development	1.33**	1.09	1.08
School Trouble	1.27***	1.12	1.13
Depression	1.62***	1.35*	1.34*
Drunkenness	1.13***	1.11***	1.11***
Drug Use	1.72***	1.53***	1.51***
Constant (Std. Error)	-3.98***	-3.72***	-3.80***
	(0.73)	(0.72)	(0.71)
F-Test	40.09***	66.55***	62.45***

* p<.05, ** p<.01, *** p<.001
a. To save space, certain weak and non-significant coefficients are not displayed, including family SES, parental supervision, tobacco use, self-esteem, unstructured socializing, and two-parent home.

Some of the relationships that were significant in Model 1 are no longer significant in Model 2, including physical development and school trouble. The other measures maintain a significant relationship with Wave Two violent victimization once prior violence is controlled for, but the strength of these associations shrinks. For example, the IRR between gender and violent victimization shrinks to 2.49 in Model 2 (exp[0.91], p-value <0.001) compared to 3.75 in Model 1.

In the third model predicting violent victimization, an interaction term between prior violent victimization (non-partner related) and IPV victimization is added. Adding the interaction term to this model resulted in an effect similar to that of the interaction term in Table 5.7. The interaction term in Model 3 in Table 5.8 indicates that individuals with the lowest levels of Wave One violent victimization experience the sharpest increase in the expected count of Wave Two violent victimization for every one-unit increase in Wave Two IPV victimization, as compared to individuals with the highest level of Wave One violent victimization. The interaction between prior violent victimization and IPV victimization (exp[-0.08] = 0.92, p-value < 0.05) results in a more modest increase in Wave Two violent victimization for individuals with the highest levels of prior violent victimization than for individuals with the lowest levels of prior violent victimization. A graph of this interaction is displayed in Figure 5.2.

Figure 5.2. Interaction between Wave One Violent Victimization and Wave Two IPV Victimization

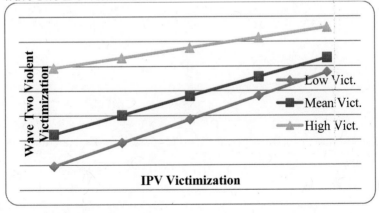

In Table 5.9, the coefficients for models predicting Wave Two general delinquency are displayed. The results of these analyses are very similar to the analyses predicting Wave Two violent offending and violent victimization. In Model 1, IPV victimization has a modest relationship with delinquency, increasing the rate of delinquency by a factor of 1.14 (beta = 0.13, p-value < 0.001). The experience of parental maltreatment as children also increases the rate of general delinquency in Wave Two (IRR = 1.11, p-value < 0.001). Gender, age, and drug use are among the strongest predictors of delinquency in this model. The rate of Wave Two delinquency for males is 1.67 times higher compared to females (b = 0.51, p-value < 0.001). An increase in age decreases the rate of delinquency by a factor of 0.83 (b = -0.18, p-value < 0.001). The rate of delinquency for adolescents who have used drugs is 1.87 times higher compared to adolescents who have not used drugs (b = 0.63, p-value < 0.001). Smoking is also positively associated with delinquency (beta = 0.07, p-value < 0.001).

In Model 2 in Table 5.9, Wave One delinquency is controlled for, and controlling for prior delinquency does not change the effect of IPV victimization. Prior delinquency has a strong relationship with Wave Two delinquency, increasing the rate of delinquency by a factor of 1.29 (b = 0.26, p-value < 0.001). IPV victimization maintains a significant, but slightly smaller effect on Wave Two delinquency (IRR = 1.12, p-value < 0.001).

Controlling for prior delinquency in Model 2 decreased the size and significance of some measures, including race (other race), school trouble, and unstructured socializing. Gender, family SES, depression, excessive drinking, smoking, and drug use maintain positive and significant relationships with delinquency in Model 2, while age and self-esteem maintain negative and significant relationships with delinquency.

In Model 3 in Table 5.9 an interaction term between prior delinquency and IPV victimization has been added. The effect of this interaction term is small (exp[-0.03] = 0.97, p-value < 0.01), but this interaction reveals that respondents who had the lowest levels of prior delinquency had the sharpest increase in Wave Two delinquency for every one-unit increase in Wave Two IPV victimization. Similar to the interactions in Tables 5.7 and 5.8, individuals with the highest levels of Wave One delinquency experience the smallest increase in Wave Two delinquency for every one-unit increase in Wave Two IPV victimization. A graph of this interaction is displayed in Figure 5.3.

Table 5.9. Negative Binomial Models Predicting Wave Two General Delinquency[a]

	Model 1	Model 2	Model 3
		IR Ratio	
Wave Two IPV Victimization	1.14***	1.12***	1.20***
Childhood Maltreatment	1.11***	0.08**	1.08**
Wave One Delinquency	--	1.29***	1.32***
Wave One Delinquency * Wave Two IPV Victimization	--	--	0.97**
Individual Characteristics			
Gender (male)	1.67***	1.38***	1.39***
Age (in years)	0.83***	0.86***	0.86***
African American	0.99	0.95	0.96
Other Race	1.26**	1.08	1.09
School Trouble	1.08*	0.96	0.97
Family SES	1.07***	1.02*	1.02*
Unstructured Socializing	1.07**	1.06	1.06*
Depression	1.40***	1.30***	1.30***
Self-Esteem	0.85***	0.90*	0.90*
Drunkenness	1.17***	1.13***	1.13***
Smoking	1.01***	1.01**	1.01**
Drug Use	1.87***	1.59***	1.59***
Constant (Std. Error)	1.88***	1.31**	1.25**
	(0.50)	(0.46)	(0.46)
F-Test	49.89***	79.78***	79.37***

* p<.05, ** p<.01, *** p<.001

a. To e space, certain weak and non-significant coefficients are not displayed, including relationship characteristics, parental supervision, and two-parent home.

Figure 5.3. Interaction between Wave One Delinquency and Wave Two IPV Victimization

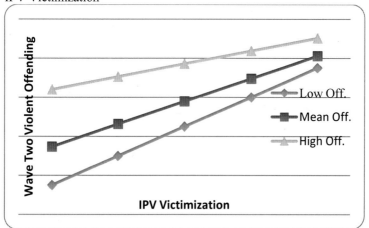

In Table 5.10, logistic regression coefficients and odds ratios predicting Wave Two drug use based on IPV victimization are displayed. In Model 1, without controlling for prior drug use, IPV victimization increases the odds of drug use by 45% (exp[0.37], p-value < 0.001). Unlike the previous models predicting violent offending and delinquency, relationship characteristics influence the likelihood of drug use. Relationships with more romantic feelings (emotional intensity) decrease the odds of drug use by 8% (exp[-0.08], p-value < 0.01). Relationships with more sexual activity, on the other hand, increase the odds of drug use (exp[0.20], p-value < 0.001).

Race also has a substantial effect on drug use. Being African American increases the odds of drug use by 53% (exp[0.42], p-value < 0.01). Adolescents who are from wealthier families, spend more time in unstructured socializing activities, drink excessively, and smoke are also more likely to use drugs. Conversely, adolescents with higher self-esteem are less likely to use drugs.

In Model 2, we observe that controlling for Wave One drug use does not substantially decrease the effect of IPV victimization. Consistent with expectations, prior drug use has the strongest effect on subsequent drug use, increasing the odds of Wave Two drug use by 288% (exp[1.36], p-value <0.001). After controlling for prior drug use,

IPV victimization increases the odds of drug use by 35% (exp[0.30], p-value < 0.01) compared to 45% in Model 1. Interaction terms between prior drug use and IPV victimization and IPV victimization and depression were also tested. However, these interaction terms were small and insignificant.

Table 5.10. Logistic Regression Models Predicting Wave Two Drug Use

	Model 1	Model 2
	Odds Ratio	
IPV Victimization	1.45***	1.35**
Childhood Maltreatment	1.07	1.04
Wave One Drug Use	--	3.88***
Relationship Characteristics		
Relationship Duration	1.04	1.03
Emotional Intensity	0.92**	0.94*
Sexual Activity	1.23***	1.17***
Individual Characteristics		
Gender (male)	1.18	1.17
Age (in years)	0.85***	0.83***
African American	1.53**	1.49*
Other Race	1.24	1.17
Physical Development	1.10	1.09
Two-Parent Home	0.88	1.00
Parental Supervision	0.88*	0.87*
Family SES	1.16***	1.13**
Unstructured Socializing	1.25***	1.23***
Depression	1.25	1.28
Self-Esteem	0.69***	0.70***
Drunkenness	1.59***	1.52***
Smoking	1.05***	1.04***
Constant (Std. Error)	0.86	1.25
	(0.85)	(0.90)
F-Test	30.51***	32.39***

* p<.05, ** p<.01, *** p<.001

In Model 2, emotional intensity still decreases the likelihood of drug use and sexual activity still increases the odds of drug use, although the size of these two effects has decreased slightly. Controlling for prior drug use does not substantially alter the effect of other predictors, including age, race, family SES and unstructured socializing.

Peer Network Influence

Given that peer deviance and having opposite sex friends are associated with one's own offending, the effects on Wave Two violent offending, violent victimization, delinquency and drug use are also tested (see Tables 5.11, 5.12, 5.13, and 5.14). Just as what was observed in Chapter 4 results, adding peer network characteristics does not influence the relationship between IPV victimization and deviance.

In Table 5.11, the effect of these peer network characteristics are small and insignificant. Mean network delinquency and violence only slightly increase violent offending, but these measures are not significant (exp[0.07]=1.07, and exp[0.05]=1.06, respectively, both non-significant). Having more opposite sex friends only slightly decreases violent offending, and this effect is also not significant (exp[-0.04] = 0.96, non-significant). The relationship between IPV victimization and prior violent offending and Wave Two violent offending was not altered by adding these peer network measures. Interaction terms between IPV victimization and peer network delinquency and violence and the proportion of opposite sex friends and gender and IPV victimization were also attempted. However, these interaction terms were small and non-significant. Because these results were not significant, they are not presented in the table.

In Table 5.12 coefficients for models predicting Wave Two violent victimization with and without peer network characteristics are displayed. As in earlier models, these peer network characteristics had no effect on Wave Two violent victimization, and controlling for these measures did not alter the relationships between any of the other measures and Wave Two violent victimization. The non-significant effect of peer network delinquency on violent victimization is weak and negative (exp[-0.04] = 0.96, non-significant), as is the effect of the proportion of opposite sex friends (exp[-0.19] = 0.83, non-significant). Mean network delinquency has a small, positive, but non-significant effect on Wave Two violent victimization (exp[0.09] = 1.09, non-significant).

Table 5.11. Negative Binomial Models Predicting Wave Two Violent
Offending with Peer Network Characteristics[a]

	Model 1	Model 2
	IR Ratio	
IPV Victimization	1.17***	1.17***
Childhood Maltreatment	1.10***	1.10***
Wave One Violent Offending	1.40***	1.40***
Wave One Violent Victimization	1.44***	1.44***
Wave One Violent Offending* IPV Victimization	0.95*	0.95*
Peer Network Characteristics		
Mean Network Delinquency	--	1.07
Mean Network Violence	--	1.06
Opposite sex friends	--	0.96
Individual Characteristics		
Gender (male)	1.88***	1.88***
Age (in years)	0.86***	0.85***
African American	1.36**	1.37**
Other Race	1.11	1.11
School Trouble	1.02	1.02
Family SES	0.91***	0.98***
Unstructured Socializing	1.04	1.04
Depression	1.41***	1.41***
Self-Esteem	1.04	1.04
Drunkenness	1.16***	1.16***
Drug Use	1.33***	1.33***
Constant (Std. Error)	-0.27	-0.33
	(0.07)	(0.58)
F-Test	61.14***	61.11***

* $p<.05$, ** $p<.01$, *** $p<.001$

a. To save space, certain weak and non-significant coefficients are not displayed, including relationship characteristics, physical development, parental support, tobacco use, and two-parent home.

Table 5.12. Negative Binomial Models Predicting Wave Two Violent Victimization with Peer Network Characteristics[a]

	Model 1	Model 2
	IR Ratio	
IPV Victimization	1.21***	1.21***
Childhood Maltreatment	1.11**	1.11**
Wave One Violent Victimization	1.97***	1.97***
Wave One Violent Offending	1.10*	1.10*
Wave One Violent Victimization * IPV Victimization	0.92*	0.92*
Peer Network Characteristics		
Mean Network Delinquency	--	0.96
Mean Network Violence	--	1.09
Opposite sex friends	--	0.83
Relationship Characteristics		
Sexual Activity	1.07*	1.07*
Individual Characteristics		
Gender (male)	2.49***	2.49***
Age (in years)	0.98	0.99
African American	1.43**	1.42**
Other Race	1.34*	1.34*
Physical Development	1.08	1.08
School Trouble	1.13	1.13
Depression	1.34*	1.34*
Drunkenness	1.11***	1.11***
Drug Use	1.51***	1.51***
Constant (Std. Error)	-3.80***	-3.97***
	(0.71)	(0.73)
F-Test	62.45***	32.12***

* p<.05, ** p<.01, *** p<.001

a. To save space, certain weak and non-significant coefficients are not displayed, including family SES, parental support, tobacco use, self-esteem, unstructured socializing, and two-parent home.

Table 5.13. Negative Binomial Models Predicting Wave Two
Delinquency with Peer Network Characteristics[a]

	Model 1	Model 2
	IR Ratio	
IPV Victimization	1.20***	1.20***
Childhood Maltreatment	1.08**	1.08**
Wave One Delinquency	1.32***	1.32***
Wave One Delinquency * IPV Victimization	0.97**	0.97**
Peer Network Characteristics		
Mean Network Delinquency	--	1.01
Mean Network Violence	--	1.09
Opposite sex friends	--	1.03
Individual Characteristics		
Gender (male)	1.39***	1.38***
Age (in years)	0.86***	0.87***
African American	0.96	0.95
Other Race	1.09	1.09
School Trouble	0.97	0.97
Family SES	1.02*	1.03*
Unstructured Socializing	1.06*	1.06*
Depression	1.30***	1.29***
Self-Esteem	0.90*	0.90*
Drunkenness	1.13***	1.13***
Smoking	1.01**	1.01**
Drug Use	1.59***	1.58***
Constant (Std. Error)	1.25**	1.08*
	(0.46)	(0.47)
F-Test	79.37***	79.12***

* p<.05, ** p<.01, *** p<.001

a. To save space, certain weak and non-significant coefficients are not displayed, including relationship characteristics, parental supervision, and two-parent home.

Table 5.14. Logistic Regression Models Predicting Wave Two Drug Use with Peer Network Characteristics

	Model 1	Model 2
	Odds Ratio	
IPV Victimization	1.35**	1.35**
Childhood Maltreatment	1.04	1.04
Wave One Drug Use	3.88***	3.79***
Peer Network Characteristics		
Mean Network Delinquency	--	1.23
Mean Network Violence	--	0.98
Opposite sex friends	--	0.86
Relationship Characteristics		
Relationship Duration	1.03	1.02
Emotional Intensity	0.94*	0.94*
Sexual Activity	1.17***	1.17***
Individual Characteristics		
Gender (male)	1.17	1.18
Age (in years)	0.83***	0.81***
African American	1.49**	1.55**
Other Race	1.17	1.17
Physical Development	1.09	1.09
Two-Parent Home	1.00	1.00
Parental Supervision	0.87*	0.88*
Family SES	1.13**	1.13**
Unstructured Socializing	1.23***	1.24***
Depression	1.28	1.27
Self-Esteem	0.70***	0.71***
Drunkenness	1.52***	1.51***
Smoking	1.04***	1.04***
Constant (Std. Error)	1.25	1.45
	(0.90)	(0.92)
F-Test	32.39***	32.40***

* $p<.05$, ** $p<.01$, *** $p<.001$

In Table 5.13, peer network characteristics again have almost no effect on Wave Two delinquency. Peer network delinquency and peer network violence are both associated with a slight, but non-significant, increase in the rate of delinquency (exp[0.01] = 1.01 and exp[0.08]=1.09, respectively, both non-significant). The effect of the proportion of opposite sex friends in the respondent's peer network is also very small, positive, and non-significant (exp[0.03] = 1.03, non-significant). Interaction terms were again attempted between prior delinquency and IPV victimization, as well as between opposite sex friends and gender and IPV victimization. Because all of these interaction terms were non-significant, they are not presented in the table.

In Table 5.14, mean network delinquency increases the odds of drug use by 23% (exp[0.21], non-significant). However, this term is insignificant. Mean peer network violence decreases the odds of drug use by only 2% (exp[-0.02], non-significant), and the proportion of opposite sex friends decreases the odds of drug use by 14% (exp[-0.15], non-significant).

Once again, interaction terms between peer network delinquency and violence and IPV victimization, as well as opposite sex friends and IPV victimization and gender were also attempted. Because all of these interaction terms were small and insignificant and did not substantially impact the model, they are not presented in the table.

Gender Differences

In the previous analyses we observed that gender had a strong influence on violent offending and delinquency, and less so on drug use. Interactions between IPV victimization and gender were included in the above analyses predicting violent offending, violent victimization, delinquency, and drug use (not displayed), and most of these interaction terms were small and non-significant. Interaction terms between gender and several other measures were also attempted, and several of these interaction terms were significant for many of the models. To further examine these interaction terms, males and females are analyzed separately in predicting Wave Two violent offending, violent victimization, delinquency, and drug use. In Tables 5.15, 5.16, 5.17, and 5.18, the coefficients for males and females are displayed separately, in addition to the z-tests for differences between coefficients. In Table 5.15, 10 significant gender differences are revealed. For example, the difference between the effect of Wave One violent victimization is significantly different between males and females ($z = -3.07$, p-value < 0.001). Prior violent victimization increases the expected count of Wave Two violent offending by 78% for females (exp[0.58], p-value < 0.001), and 30% for males (exp[0.26], p-value < 0.001).

Table 5.15. Negative Binomial Models Predicting Wave Two Violent Offending for Males and Females Separately[a]

	Males	Females	Z-Test
	IR Ratio		
IPV Victimization	1.05	1.13**	-1.36
Childhood Maltreatment	1.08**	1.12**	-1.12
Wave One Violent Offending	1.32***	1.38***	-0.35
Wave One Violent Victimization	1.30***	1.78***	-3.07***
Individual Characteristics			
Age (in years)	0.88***	0.83***	3.57***
African American	1.15	1.75***	-3.01***
Two-Parent Home	1.18	1.02	-1.19
Parental Supervision	1.01	0.94	2.92**
Family SES	0.92**	0.89*	1.67*
Unstructured Socializing	1.03	1.01	0.91
Depression	1.25*	1.50**	-2.26**
Self-Esteem	0.94	1.08	-1.92*
Drunkenness	1.12***	1.22***	-4.74***
Smoking	1.00	1.01	32.36***
Drug Use	1.35***	1.29*	-2.01*
Constant (Std. Error)	0.52	0.07	
	(0.64)	(0.97)	
F-Test	32.36***	33.34***	

* p<.05, ** p<.01, *** p<.001
a. To save space, certain weak and insignificant coefficients are not displayed including relationship characteristics and physical development.

Other significant differences between males and females include age, race, family SES, depression, excessive drinking, and drug use. Age decreases the rate of violent offending for both males and females, but this effect is significantly larger for females (exp[-0.18] = 0.83 for females, and exp[-0.13]=0.88 for males, p-value < 0.001). Being African American has a much stronger association with violent offending for females than for males. This finding is surprising, considering that African American males tend to have a higher rate of violence than other groups. Coming from a wealthier family is associated with less violent offending for females than for males.

The positive association between depression, drinking, and drug use and violent offending is also stronger for females compared to males, and all of these differences are significant. The difference between coefficients for parental supervision, self-esteem, and smoking for males and females are also significant. However, the coefficients for these measures within each of the models for males and females are not significant.

The effect of IPV victimization is slightly different for males and females, although the difference between these coefficients for the two groups is not significant (z = -1.36, non-significant). Victimization by an intimate partner increases the expected count of Wave Two violent offending by 13% for females (exp[0.12], p-value < 0.01), and only 5% for males (exp[0.05],non-significant).

According to the z-tests in Table 5.16, there are six significant differences in the effects of measures for males and females in predicting Wave Two violent victimization. These differences include the effects of Wave Two IPV victimization, Wave One violent victimization, age, unstructured socializing, smoking and drug use. Being victimized by an intimate partner is associated with a much larger increase in the rate of violent victimization for females compared to males (z = -1.84, p-value < 0.05). Being victimized by an intimate partner at Wave Two increases the expected count of Wave Two non-partner related violent victimization by 21% for females (exp[0.19], p-value < 0.01), and only 4% for males (exp[0.04], non-significant). Additionally, Wave One violent victimization increases the expected count of Wave Two violent victimization by 256% for females (exp[0.94], p-value < 0.001), compared to only 66% for males (exp[0.51], p-value < 0.001).

Table 5.16. Negative Binomial Models Predicting Wave Two Violent Victimization for Males and Females Separately[a]

	Males	Females	Z-Test
	IR Ratio		
IPV Victimization	1.04	1.21**	-1.84*
Childhood Maltreatment	1.13**	1.06	0.20
Wave One Violent Victimization	1.66***	2.56***	-4.03***
Wave One Violent Offending	1.09	1.08	-0.01
Relationship Characteristics			
Sexual Activity	1.06	1.14*	-1.06
Individual Characteristics			
Age (in years)	1.03	0.91	1.65*
African American	1.33*	1.56*	-0.75
Two-Parent Home	1.15	0.81	1.51
School Trouble	1.20*	0.98	1.51
Family SES	0.96	0.98	-0.44
Unstructured Socializing	1.04	1.25**	-2.08*
Depression	1.35*	1.21	0.47
Drunkenness	1.08**	1.13*	-0.59
Smoking	1.01	0.99	1.92*
Drug Use	1.33*	1.98***	-1.89*
Constant (Std. Error)	-3.21***	-3.01*	
	(0.83)	(1.29)	
F-Test	29.18***	29.30***	

* p<.05, ** p<.01, *** p<.001

a. To save space, certain weak and insignificant coefficients are not displayed including the duration and emotional intensity of the relationship.

Table 5.17 reveals only two significant differences between males and females in predicting Wave Two delinquent behavior. One significant difference is the effect of prior delinquency, which is larger for females than for males (exp[0.31]=1.37 and exp[0.22]=1.24, respectively, p-value < 0.001) and the difference between these two coefficients is significant (z = -2.74, p-value < 0.001). The difference between the coefficients for IPV victimization is not significant. The effect of IPV victimization is only slightly larger for females compared to males (exp[0.15]=1.17 and exp[0.09]=1.09, respectively, both p-values < 0.01).

The only other major difference between males and females in predicting Wave Two delinquency is the effect of excessive drinking. Excessive drinking increased the expected count of delinquency by 21% for females (exp[0.19], p-value < 0.001), and only 7% for males (exp[0.06], p-value < 0.05). The difference between these two coefficients for males and females is significant (z = -3.51, p-value < 0.001).

Table 5.17. Negative Binomial Models Predicting Wave Two Delinquency for Males and Females Separately[a]

	Males	Females	Z-Test
	IR Ratio		
IPV Victimization	1.09**	1.17***	-0.34
Childhood Maltreatment	1.09*	1.05*	0.47
Wave One Delinquency	1.24***	1.37***	-2.74**
Individual Characteristics			
Age (in years)	0.89***	0.87***	1.52
African American	0.84	1.07	-1.59
Other Race	1.03	1.14	-0.39
School Trouble	0.97	0.99	-0.09
Family SES	1.03	1.03	0.50
Unstructured Socializing	1.06	1.05	0.07
Depression	1.17	1.37**	-1.17
Self-Esteem	0.87	0.94	-0.05
Drunkenness	1.07*	1.21***	-3.51***
Smoking	1.01*	1.01	-0.10
Drug Use	1.69***	1.39***	1.35
Constant (Std. Error)	1.34	1.32**	
	(0.72)	(0.50)	
F-Test	35.57***	55.69***	

* p<.05, ** p<.01, *** p<.001

a. To save space, certain weak and insignificant coefficients are not displayed including relationship characteristics and physical development.

In the models predicting Wave Two drug use for males and females separately in Table 5.18 there is only one significant difference between these two groups: the effect of race ($z = 2.01$, p-value < 0.05). Being African American increases the odds of drug use by 211% for males (exp[0.75], p-value < 0.01) and only 6% for females (exp[0.06], p-value > 0.05).

Table 5.18. Logistic Regression Models Predicting Wave Two Drug Use for Males and Female Separately[a]

	Males	**Females**	**Z-Test**
	Odds Ratio		
IPV Victimization	1.33	1.35*	-0.09
Childhood Maltreatment	1.03	1.03	0.01
Wave One Drug Use	3.91***	3.85***	0.06
Relationship Characteristics			
Relationship Duration	1.08	0.97	1.13
Emotional Intensity	0.96	0.92*	0.76
Sexual Activity	1.17**	1.18**	-0.14
Individual Characteristics			
Age (in years)	0.88*	0.80***	1.19
African American	2.11**	1.06	2.01*
Parental Supervision	0.87	0.88	-0.06
Family SES	1.21**	1.06	-1.43
Unstructured Socializing	1.12	1.33***	-1.49
Depression	1.05	1.40	-1.00
Self-Esteem	0.69*	0.73*	-0.28
Drunkenness	1.43***	1.61***	-1.59
Smoking	1.04***	1.04***	0.26
Constant (Std. Error)	0.08	1.93	
	(1.24)	(1.18)	
F-Test	15.67***	26.55***	

* p<.05, ** p<.01, *** p<.001

a. To save space, certain weak and insignificant coefficients are not displayed including school trouble and physical development.

The effect of IPV victimization for males and females is almost identical; IPV victimization increases the odds of drug use by 33% for males (exp[0.28], p-value > 0.05) and 35% for females (exp[0.30], p-value < 0.05), although this effect is significant for females and not for males. The difference between these two coefficients is not significant (z = -0.09, p-value > 0.05). The effect of prior drug use is also nearly identical for males and females. Prior drug use increases the odds of Wave Two drug use by 391% for males (exp[1.36], p-value < 0.001) and 385% for females (exp[1.35], p-value < 0.001). However, the difference between these two coefficients is not significant (z = 0.06, p-value > 0.05).

Summary of Results

The above analyses reveal, contrary to what was expected based on Agnew's general strain theory (GST), that gender does not moderate the relationship between IPV victimization and drug use. Based on Agnew's GST, we would also expect that depression mediates the effect of IPV victimization on these outcomes, particularly drug use for females. That is, we would expect the effect of IPV victimization on drug use to work through depression. To test for whether depression mediated the relationship between IPV victimization and deviant behavior for males and/or females, depression was added and removed from analyses. There was no evidence that depression mediates the relationship between IPV victimization and drug use for males or females, nor did it mediate the relationships between IPV victimization and any of the other outcome measures. Depression was not a significant predictor of drug use for males or females. The size of the effect of depression appeared to be much larger for females as compared to males (odds ratios = 1.05 and 1.40, respectively, p-value > 0.05), but this difference was not significant.

Peer network characteristics (mean peer network delinquency and violence and the proportion of opposite sex friends) were also added to all of the above analyses for males and females. These results were consistent with results reported in Chapter 4, in which peer network characteristics did not influence the outcomes (violent offending, violent victimization, delinquency, and drug use). Nor did interaction terms including these measures influence the outcomes. Angew's GST would have predicted that having deviant peer networks would further aggravate the effects of IPV victimization. Also, for females, having more male friends could moderate the effect of IPV victimization. However, all of these interaction terms were small in size and insignificant. Peer network characteristics do not appear to influence the odds of IPV victimization, nor the behaviors that are associated with it.

CONCLUSIONS

The above results revealed four main findings. First, short-term violent offending, violent victimization, delinquency, and drug use are all associated with IPV victimization. More importantly, even after controlling for prior occurrences of each of these behaviors, and several other pertinent variables, the effect of IPV victimization remained. IPV victimization is associated with an increase in violent offending, violent victimization, delinquency, and drug use.

Second, peer network characteristics do not influence or moderate these relationships. Although peer network delinquency and violence are associated with all three of these outcomes at the bivariate level, in the multivariate analyses the effects of these measures were weak and insignificant. The interaction terms with these measures and IPV victimization were also negligible.

Third, there were a few key gender differences and similarities in the relationship between IPV victimization and deviant behaviors. The effect of IPV victimization on violent offending and delinquency was slightly larger for females as compared to males, although the differences between these coefficients were not significant. Past violent victimization was also a stronger predictor of violent offending for females compared to males, and this difference was significant. Overall, my finding that recent and past victimization is a stronger predictor of offending for females than for males is consistent with past research. Many female gang members have been the victims of both childhood abuse and relationship violence (Miller 2001). Overall, victimization is a salient predictor of offending for females, and these results are further evidence of that.

Another key gender finding is that IPV victimization was a significant predictor of all three outcomes, even violent offending and drug use. Following Agnew's GST, and the research of Broidy and Agnew (1997) based on GST, we would expect that females would be less likely to engage in violence as a result of IPV victimization compared to male victims, and more likely to engage in drug use. However, the results revealed that IPV victimization was a significant and much larger predictor of violent offending for females compared to males and males and females were about equally likely to use drugs as a result of IPV victimization.

Additionally, the effect of depression was not significantly different for males and females. Depression was a larger predictor of violent offending, delinquency, and drug use for females compared to males. However, these effects were not significantly different between the two groups. Moreover, depression did not moderate or mediate the relationship between IPV victimization and these outcomes, as expected based on Agnew's GST.

Lastly, peer network characteristics did not have a substantial influence on the three outcomes (violent offending, delinquency, and drug use) after controlling for other relevant factors. Nor did these measures moderate the relationship between IPV victimization and these outcomes, as strain theory would have predicted. Also notable, the effect of opposite sex peer networks did not influence the outcomes for either males or females, and this measure did not moderate the relationship between IPV victimization and deviant behaviors, as expected based on Agnew's GST.

Overall, the relationship between IPV victimization and deviance is similar to that of general violent victimization and deviant behaviors. General violent victimization is related to subsequent deviant behaviors, including violent offending, delinquency, and drug use. As suggested by the results in Chapter 4, these results in Chapter 5 also suggest that IPV victimization shares some characteristics with general violent victimization.

In the next chapter of results, mutual and one-sided IPV victimization are distinguished. These different types of IPV victimization may each be more similar to or distinct from general violent victimization. The distinction between mutual and one-sided IPV victimization is used to examine whether the risk factors and associated deviant behaviors vary depending on whether the IPV victimization was mutual or one-sided.

CHAPTER 6

The Causes and Correlates of Mutual and One-Sided Adolescent Intimate Partner Violence

INTRODUCTION

In the two prior chapters Add Health survey data were used to assess the causes and correlates of adolescent IPV. In this chapter IPV is divided into two categories; IPV victimization that was reported by only one individual in the couple (one-sided) and IPV victimization that was reported by both partners in the couple (mutual). By creating this distinction between one-sided and mutual IPV victimization, this research provides an approximate replication of Johnson's (2008) typology of IPV. One-sided abuse represents c, and mutual abuse represents situational couple violence[5].

The purpose of making the distinction between mutual and one-sided abuse is to determine whether risk factors and correlates of IPV vary based on this distinction. Despite research showing that multiple types of IPV exist, all research and theory on IPV assumes one type of abuse: intimate terrorism (Johnson and Ferraro 2000). As Johnson

---

[5] It is important to note that these types do not fully represent Johnson's typology of IPV. First, all of Johnson's categories of IPV are not included (i.e., violent resistance and mutual violent control are not). Second, these measures lack context. In other words, IPV that has been coded as mutual IPV could represent both situational couple violence and violent resistance. Also, IPV that has been coded as one-sided could be situational couple violence.

(2008) and other researchers have found, IPV may also consist of mutual aggression (for a full review, see Archer 2000). Theory and research that do not make the distinction between different types of IPV fail to provide a complete picture of partner abuse. In this chapter the risk factors and correlates of both one-sided and mutual IPV are examined.

The analyses and results presented in this chapter are divided into three main sections. First, this chapter provides a description of the sample and measures used in these analyses. Second, the following two bivariate relationships are examined: (1) Wave One violence and IPV victimization; and, (2) IPV victimization and Wave Two violent offending, violent victimization, delinquency. In the final section of this chapter, the multivariate results are presented and discussed.

In the first part of the multivariate analyses, Wave One violent offending and violent victimization are first used to predict a categorical measure of IPV victimization using multinomial regression. The categorical measure of IPV victimization represents no IPV victimization (reference category), mutual IPV victimization, and one-sided IPV victimization. These analyses are single-level. In other words, each couple occupies a single row of data. Both characteristics of the female partners and the male partners are used to predict the categorical outcome.

In the next part of the multivariate analyses, Hierarchical Linear Modeling (HLM) is used to analyze nested couple data. That is, each of the 440 respondents are nested within 220 couples. Individual characteristics along with couple-level characteristics are used to predict Wave Two violent offending, violent victimization (non-partner related), delinquency, and drug use. At the couple-level, IPV victimization is divided into four categories: (1) no IPV victimization (reference category); (2) mutual IPV victimization; (3) one-sided IPV victimization with a female victim; and, (4) one-sided IPV victimization with a male victim.

In these analyses, a Poisson distribution that takes into account the over-dispersion of the dependent variables is used to predict Wave Two violent offending, violent victimization, and delinquency. In the analyses predicting Wave Two drug use, logistic regression is used (the

Bernoulli distribution in HLM). The data used and analytic strategies used will be explained in more detail below.

THE SAMPLE AND DESCRIPTIVE STATISTICS

The data used in this chapter are unlike the data used in Chapters 4 and 5, which used Add Health data to examine the causes and correlates of IPV for all reported abuse. The data used in this chapter also come from the Add Health survey, but the respondents analyzed in this study are limited to reciprocated romantic partner nominations taken during the Wave Two interview. That is, the data used in this chapter of results include only respondents within couples who nominated one another as romantic partners and who were linked by the survey administrators.

As described in Chapter 3 of this monograph, respondents could identify their romantic and non-romantic partners from the list of other respondents included in the Add Health survey. If the identified partners participated in the second wave of interviews, couples could be matched and data could be extracted from both partners within the couple. A total of 865 couples (or 1,730 individual respondents) could be matched, but only 220 of these partnerships were recognized by both individuals within the couple. Information from these matched couples (220 couples, 440 individual respondents) comprise the data used in this chapter.

To preserve an adequate sample size, these data are not subject to the same limitations as the data used in Chapters 4 and 5. This sample is not limited to respondents who were 18-years-old and younger during the second wave interview. Also, the parental maltreatment and peer network characteristics measures have been eliminated. To keep the parental maltreatment measure in the analyses, the sample would have been limited to respondents present in all three waves of data, which could have further reduced this already small sample. Also, the peer network measures were eliminated due to the high rate of missing data in these measures. To ensure that other missing data do not limit the sample size, multiple imputation was used for all of the measures in these analyses.

A descriptive account of the Wave Two dependent variables and their Wave One counterparts are displayed in Table 6.1. The prevalence of Wave Two IPV victimization in this sample is similar to the sample used in the previous two Chapters (see Table 4.1 on page 95 for a comparison). Based on the count measures of IPV victimization at Wave Two, the respondents in this sample experienced an average of 0.48 out of 5 types of IPV victimization (all IPV), 0.38 out of 3 types of verbal abuse, and 0.10 out of 2 types of physical abuse. Based on the binary measures of IPV victimization, a slightly larger proportion of this sample experienced any verbal IPV victimization compared to the sample used in Chapters 4 and 5. Thirty-two percent of this sample experienced any type of IPV victimization, 29% experienced any type of verbal victimization, and 9% experienced physical victimization (compared to 27%, 25%, and 9%, respectively, in the previous sample).

A descriptive account of the number of respondents who experienced mutual and one-sided IPV victimization is also displayed in Table 6.1. Of the 32% of the sample who experienced any type of IPV victimization, a little less than half (or 14% of the whole sample) were in relationships in which both partners in the couple reported victimization, and a little more than half (or 18% of the entire sample) were in relationships where only one person reported IPV victimization and his or her partner did not.

This sample also has similar amounts of violent offending, violent victimization, and delinquency compared to the previous sample. As can be seen in Table 6.1, respondents had more violent offending in Wave One (0.56 out of a possible 5 offenses) than in Wave Two (0.35 offenses). Violent victimizations also declined in Wave One compared to Wave Two. Respondents reported an average of 0.44 out of a possible 4 violent victimizations in Wave One, compared to an average of 0.21 in Wave Two. Involvement in general delinquency also declined in Wave Two compared to Wave One. Respondents committed an average of 1.22 out of a possible 9 delinquent acts in Wave One, compared to 0.81 in Wave Two.

Unlike violence and delinquency, the prevalence of drug use increased slightly between Waves One and Two. Twenty percent of the sample reported any type of drug use in Wave One, and 21% reported drug use in Wave Two. The proportion of respondents who used drugs in this sample is very similar compared to the sample of respondents used in Chapters 4 and 5.

Table 6.1. Descriptive Statistics: IPV, Violent Offending, Violent Victimization, General Delinquency, and Drug Use

Variable	Mean/ Percent	Std Dev	Range
Wave Two IPV Victimization - Count			
Any	0.48	0.84	0 - 5
Verbal	0.38	0.67	0 - 3
Physical	0.10	0.32	0 - 2
Wave Two IPV Victimization - Binary			
Any	32%	--	--
Verbal	29%	--	--
Physical	9%	--	--
IPV Types—Level One			
Any Abuse	14%	--	--
Verbal Abuse	18%	--	--
IPV Types—Level Two			
Mutual	14%	--	--
One-Sided with Female Victim	15%	--	--
One-Sided with Male Victim	21%	--	--
Violent Offending			
Wave One Violent Offending	0.56	0.95	0 - 5
Wave Two Violent Offending	0.35	0.84	0 – 5
Violent Victimization			
Wave One Violent Victimization	0.44	0.75	0 - 4
Wave Two Violent Victimization	0.21	0.63	0 - 4
General Delinquency			
Wave One Delinquency	1.22	1.67	0 - 9
Wave Two Delinquency	0.81	1.44	0 - 9
Wave Two IPV Victimization - Binary			
Wave One Drug Use	20%	--	--
Wave Two Drug Use	21%	--	--

Level One N = 440, Level Two N = 220

Note: The count versions of IPV victimization are used as independent measures in the second section of analyses in this chapter. Also, the Wave One versions of violent offending, violent victimization, general delinquency, and drug use are also used as independent measures in the first and second set of analyses.

Descriptions of the control variables are displayed in Table 6.2. Based on the characteristics displayed in this table, this sample is very similar to the sample used in Chapters 4 and 5. Given that this sample comprises heterosexual couples, exactly one half is male and the other female. A slightly smaller proportion of this sample is non-white compared to the previous sample: 13% African American and 17% from other non-white races and ethnicities). Because this sample is not limited to respondents 18 years of age or younger, the age range in this sample is slightly higher (13 to 21). The average age is slightly higher at 16.73.

Because part of the data used in these analyses are nested (individual respondents are nested within couples), relationship characteristics are used as level two measures in the HLM analyses. Duration, emotional intensity, and sexual activity are aggregate measures based on the responses from each individual within each couple. The averages for these relationship characteristics are very similar to the level one measures used in the previous analyses. The average length of these relationships was a little over one year (1.05 years). Of the ten possible non-sexual activities the respondents could have engaged in with their partners (e.g., meet each other's parents, exchange gifts), they engaged in an average of 6.76 of these activities. Respondents engaged in about 2.29 of the 4 possible sexual activities on average (e.g., talk about contraceptives, touched each other's genitals).

In Table 6.3, descriptive statistics for the male and female partners used in this Chapter are listed separately. Surprisingly, the males in this sample experienced slightly more IPV victimization, on average. Thirty-five percent of the males in this sample reported experiencing any type of IPV victimization, compared to 28% of the females. Given that this is a sample of matched male and female partners, the same proportion of each gender reported mutual IPV victimization. However, a larger proportion of the male respondents reported being the victim of one-sided IPV (22% compared to 14%).

Consistent with expectations, males reported more instances of both violent offending and violent victimization. The male respondents also reported a higher average of delinquency, and a larger proportion of the male sample used drugs. For the other control variables used in this study, males and females were very similar. The males in this sample were slightly older than the females (17-years-old, compared to 16-years-old).

Table 6.2. Descriptive Statistics for Control Variables

Variable	Mean/ Percent	Std Dev	Range
Level One Measures			
Male	50%		
African American	13%		
Other Race	17%		
Physical Development	65%		
Two-Parent Home	68%		
Age (In Years, Wave Two)	16.73	1.32	13 - 21
Family Socioeconomic Status	3.06	1.26	0 - 5
Unstructured Socializing	2.13	0.91	0 - 3
Drunkenness	0.91	1.40	0 - 6
Tobacco Use	6.97	11.72	0 - 30
Parental Supervision	3.55	0.99	1 - 5
Depression	0.57	0.37	0 - 3
Self-Esteem	4.18	0.53	1 - 5
School Trouble	2.31	0.66	1 - 5
Level Two Measures—Relationship Characteristics			
Duration (In Years)	1.05	0.95	0 - 1.66
Emotional Intensity	6.76	1.53	0 - 10
Sexual Activity	2.29	1.13	0 - 4

Level One N = 440, Level Two N = 220

BIVARIATE RESULTS: THE PREVALENCE OF WAVE TWO IPV VICTIMIZATION, VIOLENT OFFENDING, VIOLENT VICTIMIZATION, DELINQUENCY, AND DRUG USE

The following bivariate analyses first examine the relationship between prior violence (i.e., Wave One violent offending and violent victimization) and mutual and one-sided IPV victimization. Then, the bivariate relationships between mutual and one-sided IPV victimization and Wave Two violent offending, violent victimization, delinquency, and drug use are presented and discussed.

Table 6.3. Descriptive Statistics for Male and Female Respondents

Variable	Males		Females	
	Mean/ Percent	Std. Dev.	Mean/ Percent	Std. Dev.
Dependent Measures				
Any IPV Victimization - Count	0.55	0.86	0.42	0.81
Any IPV Victimization - Binary	35%		28%	
Mutual IPV Victimization	14%		14%	
One-Sided IPV Victimization	22%		14%	
Wave Two Violent Offending	0.52	1.02	0.17	0.54
Wave Two Violent Victimization	0.36	0.82	0.05	0.26
Wave Two Delinquency	0.93	1.55	0.69	1.32
Wave Two Drug Use	25%		17%	
Independent Measures				
African American	14%		11%	
Other Race	15%		19%	
Physical Development	64%		66%	
Two-Parent Home	71%		65%	
Age in Years (Wave Two)	17	1.24	16	1.31
Family Socioeconomic Status	3.12	1.30	3.00	1.21
Unstructured Socializing	2.15	0.90	2.10	0.92
Drunkenness	1.08	1.50	0.74	1.27
Tobacco Use	7.39	12.11	6.54	11.31
Parental Supervision	3.57	1.02	3.54	0.96
Depression	0.55	0.34	0.59	0.39
Self-Esteem	4.23	0.52	4.13	0.53
School Trouble	2.32	0.64	2.31	0.67
Relationship Characteristics				
Duration (years)	1.08	1.19	1.02	0.90
Emotional Intensity	6.52	2.37	7.00	1.75
Sexual Activity	2.23	1.38	2.34	1.34

Level One N = 440, Level Two N = 220

Wave One Violence and IPV Victimization

Displayed in Table 6.4 are the correlation coefficients between three types of Wave Two IPV victimization (any abuse, mutual IPV victimization, and one-sided IPV victimization, measured at Wave Two) and Wave One violent offending and violent victimization. As can be seen in this table, all of these measures are positively, but not strongly, correlated. The correlation between any type of IPV victimization and violent offending is the largest ($r = 0.24$, p-value < 0.001). Unexpectedly, mutual IPV victimization has the weakest correlation with Wave One violence. It was expected that individuals in mutually aggressive relationships would have a history of violence, especially violent offending.

Tables 6.5 and 6.6 describe the prevalence of Wave One violent offending and violent victimization with Wave Two IPV victimization (any IPV victimization, mutual IPV victimization, and one-sided IPV victimization). These frequencies represent how often prior violent offending and violent victimization overlapped with measures of Wave Two IPV victimization. The purpose of these tables is to gain an understanding of how often different types of IPV victimization co-occur.

First, looking at Table 6.5, of the 66% of the sample who did not engage in violent offending in Wave One, 24% (16% of the total sample) were IPV victims in Wave Two (top of the table). In contrast, of the 34% of the sample who did engage in violent offending at Wave One, 47% (16% of the entire sample) were IPV victims in Wave Two.

This pattern is consistent across all three types of IPV victimization. Of the 66% of the sample who did not engage in violent offending at Wave One, 11% (7% of the total sample) were also victims of IPV at Wave Two (middle of Table 6.5). In contrast, of the 34% of the sample who engaged in violent offending at Wave One, 21% (7% of the total sample) were also victims of IPV at Wave Two. Looking at the bottom of Table 6.5, of the 34% of the sample who engaged in violent offending at Wave One, 26% (9% of the total sample) were also victims of IPV at Wave Two. The difference between these groups is statistically significant. The premise of these analyses is that individuals in mutually violent relationships should have a history of violence, especially violent offending. However, as these tables suggest, both victims of mutual IPV and one-sided IPV have similar prevalence of past violent offending. In fact, a slightly larger proportion of violent offenders are also the victims of one-sided IPV.

Table 6.4. Correlation Coefficients—Violent Offending, Violent Victimization, and IPV Victimization

Wave Two Measure Of IPV Victimization	Wave One Violence	
	Violent Offending	Violent Victimization
Any Abuse	0.24***	0.19***
Mutual Victimization	0.12***	0.04***
One-Sided Victimization	0.18***	0.19***

Displaying Pearson's R Correlations
N = 440
* p<.05, ** p<.01, *** p<.001

Based on Table 6.6, we observe that violent victimization overlaps with all three types of IPV victimization. Of the 68% of the sample who were not victimized by general violence (i.e., non-partner related) at Wave One, 25% (17% of the entire sample) were victims of IPV at Wave Two. In contrast, of the 32% of the sample who were victims of general violence at Wave Two, 44% (14% of the total sample) were also victimized by their partners at Wave Two.

Referencing the middle of Table 6.6, we see that a slightly different pattern emerges for mutual and one-sided IPV victimization. Of the 69% of the sample who were not victims of general violence at Wave One, 13% (9% of the sample) were victims of mutual IPV at Wave Two. Of the 31% of the sample who were victims of general violence at Wave One, 16% (5% of the total sample) were also victims of mutual IPV at Wave Two. These figures are smaller compared to the overlap between general violent victimization and any type of IPV victimization. Referencing the bottom of Table 6.6, of the 32% of the sample who were victims of general violence at Wave One, 28% (9% of the total sample) were also victims of one-sided IPV at Wave Two. This proportion is much larger compared to the overlap between general violent victimization and mutual IPV victimization. This research expects that victims of one-sided IPV have a history of general violent victimization, given that victims tend to be victims again. In this case, past violent victimization appears to overlap more with one-sided IPV victimization compared to mutual IPV victimization, which is consistent with expectations. Based on a comparison of the frequencies displayed in Tables 6.5 and 6.6, it appears that these three phenomena often co-occur in this sample. That is, respondents involved in Wave One violent offending and Wave Two IPV victimization are also likely to be involved in Wave One violent victimization and Wave Two IPV victimization.

Table 6.5. Prevalence of Wave One Violent Offending and Any, Mutual and One-Sided Wave Two IPV Victimization

	Percentage of Adolescents Reporting:	
	No – Any IPV Victimization	Yes – Any IPV Victimization
No - Wave One Offending	50%	16%
Yes - Wave One Offending	18%	16%
Phi Coefficient	0.24**	
	No – Mutual IPV Victimization	Yes – Mutual IPV Victimization
No - Wave One Offending	59%	7%
Yes - Wave One Offending	27%	7%
Phi Coefficient	0.12***	
	No – One-Sided IPV Victimization	Yes – One-Sided IPV Victimization
No - Wave One Offending	57%	9%
Yes - Wave One Offending	25%	9%
Phi Coefficient	0.18***	

N = 440
Difference between groups significant at $*p < 0.05$, $**p < 0.01$, $***p < 0.001$

Table 6.6. Prevalence of Wave One Violent Offending and Any, Mutual and One-Sided Wave Two IPV Victimization

Percentage of Adolescents Reporting:		
	No – Any IPV Victimization	Yes – Any IPV Victimization
No - Wave One Victimization	51%	17%
Yes - Wave One Victimization	18%	14%
Phi Coefficient	0.19**	
	No – Mutual IPV Victimization	Yes – Mutual IPV Victimization
No - Wave One Victimization	60%	9%
Yes - Wave One Victimization	26%	5%
Phi Coefficient	0.04**	
	No – One-Sided IPV Victimization	Yes – One-Sided IPV Victimization
No - Wave One Victimization	60%	9%
Yes - Wave One Victimization	23%	9%
Phi Coefficient	0.19***	

N = 440
Difference between groups significant at *p < 0.05, **p < 0.01, ***p < 0.001

In Table 6.7, the prevalence of both Wave One violence and Wave Two IPV victimization together has been divided between males and females to see how often these phenomena occur for these two groups. As expected, a larger proportion of male respondents as compared to female respondents have engaged in prior violent offending and have been the victims of prior general violence. The difference between these groups is statistically significant.

Similar proportions of males and females were the victims of IPV (all, mutual, and one-sided), although a larger proportion of male respondents have been the victims of any type of IPV (18% for males compared to 14% for females) and one-sided IPV (11% for males compared to 7% of females). This finding may appear to be inconsistent with Johnson's (2008) research on IPV victimization, which has found that females are more likely to be the sole victims of IPV (i.e., intimate terrorism). However, we must keep in mind that Add Health's IPV victimization scale includes a large proportion of less serious forms of IPV victimization (i.e., verbal abuse). Given that this data set is comprised of matched male and female partners, the same number of male and female respondents reported mutual IPV victimization.

Table 6.7. Prevalence of Wave One Violent Offending, General Violent Victimization, and Wave Two IPV Victimization (Mutual and One-Sided) for Adolescent Males and Females

	Male		Female
Yes – W1 Violent Offender	23%		11%
No – W1 Violent Offender	27%		39%
Phi Coefficient		0.25***	
Yes – W1 Violent Victim	22%		9%
No – W1 Violent Victim	28%		41%
Phi Coefficient		0.29***	
Yes – W2 IPV Victim, All	18%		14%
No – W2 IPV Victim, All	32%		36%
Phi Coefficient		0.08***	
Yes – W2 IPV Victim, Mutual	7%		7%
No – W2 IPV Victim, Mutual	43%		43%
Phi Coefficient		0.00	
Yes – W2 IPV Victim, One-Sided	11%		7%
No – W2 IPV Victim, One-Sided	39%		43%
Phi Coefficient		0.01***	

N = 440

Difference between groups significant at *p < 0.05, **p < 0.01, ***p < 0.001

Wave Two IPV Victimization and Wave Two Deviant Behavior

In Table 6.8, correlation coefficients between Wave Two IPV victimization and four types of Wave Two deviant behavior (violent offending, violent victimization, delinquency, and drug use) are displayed. All of these correlation coefficients are positive, significant, but weak. Although all of the correlation coefficients for any type of IPV victimization and the four types of deviant behavior are small in size, the correlations between any type of IPV victimization and violent offending and violent victimization are smaller compared to delinquency and drug use.

The size of the correlations between mutual IPV victimization and these deviant behaviors is consistent across all four types of deviant behaviors (Pearson's r ranges from 0.12 to 0.13). One-sided IPV victimization has a stronger relationship with delinquency and drug use as compared to violent offending and violent victimization (although, again, all of these correlations are weak). That one-sided IPV victimization has a stronger relationship with drug use as compared to violent offending is consistent with expectations. We would expect that victims of one-sided IPV would be more prone to self-destructive behaviors rather than violent behaviors. Given that victims tend to be re-victimized, we would expect that one-sided IPV victimization would have a stronger relationship with general victimization, but it does not.

Table 6.8. Correlation Coefficients—Wave Two IPV Victimization (Mutual and One-Sided), and Wave Two Violent Offending, Violent Victimization, General Delinquency, and Drug Use

W2 IPV Victim Type	W2 Violent Offending	W2 Violent Victimization	W2 Delinquency	W2 Drug Use
Any Victimization	0.13***	0.13***	0.19***	0.19***
Mutual Victimization	0.13***	0.12***	0.13***	0.12***
One-Sided Victimization	0.04*	0.05**	0.12***	0.12***

Displaying Pearson's R Correlations

N = 440

* p<.05, ** p<.01, *** p<.001

Table 6.9. Prevalence of Wave One and Wave Two Violent Offending, Violent Victimization, General Delinquency, and Drug Use Across Three Types of IPV Victimization

	Percentage of Adolescents Reporting:		
	Violent Offending		
	Wave One	Wave Two	Both Waves
W2 IPV	16%	8%	6%
W2 IPV – Mutual	7%	4%	3%
W2 IPV – One-Sided	9%	4%	3%
	Violent Victimization		
	Wave One	Wave Two	Both Waves
W2 IPV	14%	6%	5%
W2 IPV – Mutual	5%	3%	3%
W2 IPV – One-Sided	9%	3%	2%
	General Delinquency		
	Wave One	Wave Two	Both Waves
W2 IPV	6%	6%	1%
W2 IPV – Mutual	2%	2%	<1%
W2 IPV – One-Sided	4%	4%	<1%
	Drug Use		
	Wave One	Wave Two	Both Waves
W2 IPV	10%	10%	6%
W2 IPV – Mutual	5%	5%	3%
W2 IPV – One-Sided	6%	6%	3%

N = 440

Table 6.9 describes the prevalence of violent offending, violent victimization, general delinquency, and drug use for all three types of IPV victimization across the first two waves of data. These frequencies represent how often these four behaviors overlapped with different types of Wave Two IPV victimization. The purpose of this table is to observe whether these phenomena overlap more or less with different types of IPV victimization.

At the top of Table 6.9 we observe that a larger proportion of the sample engaged in violent offending at Wave One and were the victims of one-sided IPV as compared to mutual IPV (7%). The same proportion of the sample (4%) engaged in violent offending at Wave Two and were the victims of mutual and one-sided IPV at Wave Two.

Only a small fraction of the overall sample engaged in violent offending during both waves of data and were the victims of IPV at Wave Two. The size of the overlap between two waves of violent offending and Wave Two IPV victimization are the same for both mutual and one-sided IPV victimization (3%). We would expect a higher proportion of victims of mutual IPV to report violent offending at both waves, but that is not the case.

In the next set of frequencies in Table 6.9, the overlap between two waves of general violent victimization and IPV victimization are displayed. A larger proportion of the sample were victims of general violence at Wave One and were the victims of one-sided IPV at Wave Two (9%), which is consistent with expectations. A very small fraction of the overall sample were victims of general violence during both waves and victims of IPV at Wave Two. This frequency is the smallest for victims of one-sided IPV (2%), which is not consistent with expectations. We would expect a large proportion of one-sided IPV victims to also be victims of general violence during both waves of data.

General delinquency appears to have the smallest overlap with all three types of IPV victimization. In the bottom middle of Table 6.9, less than 1% of the entire sample engaged in general delinquency during both waves of data and were the victims of either mutual or one-sided IPV. Thus, in this sample of data, general delinquency does not appear to have a strong relationship with any type of IPV victimization (including mutual and one-sided IPV victimization).

Based on the figures displayed in the bottom of Table 6.9, a larger proportion of the sample used drugs during both waves of data and were the victims of IPV. A larger proportion of the sample used drugs and were the victims of one-sided IPV at Wave One and Wave Two, but the same proportion of the sample used drugs and were the victims of mutual and one-sided abuse for both waves of data. We would have expected a larger overlap between one-sided IPV victimization and drug use compared to mutual IPV victimization, but this did not occur.

MULTIVARIATE RESULTS

In this section of the chapter the multivariate results are displayed and discussed in two parts. In the first part, multinomial regression was used to predict a categorical measure of IPV victimization based on prior violence (both offending and victimization). This measure represents (a) no IPV victimization, (b) mutual IPV victimization, and (c) one-sided IPV victimization. These analyses used a wide version of the romantic partner network data. Each couple was listed on a single line of data, and both characteristics of the male and female partners were used to predict the couple-level outcome (mutual or one-sided IPV victimization).

In the second section of multivariate analyses, binary measures of mutual and one-sided IPV victimization were used to predict same-wave violent offending, violent victimization, delinquency, and drug use, controlling for prior instances of these behaviors. These analyses were conducted using a long and nested version of the romantic partner data. These data comprise two levels. In the first level of data, each of the 440 individuals are listed on a single line of data. The second level of data contains couple-level characteristics, including whether one or both of the individuals in each couple experienced IPV victimization. Because these data are nested, HLM is used for analysis. As noted in Chapter 3, respondents nested within the same relationships are likely to be more similar to one another than to respondents nested in other relationships meaning the data likely violate the assumption of independent errors. By using HLM, it is possible to correct for this dependence problem and examine how both relationship characteristics and individual characteristics influence the above outcomes simultaneously.

Wave One Violence and Mutual and One-Sided IPV Victimization

The outcome measure in this section of the analysis is a categorical measure of mutual and one-sided IPV victimization. Multinomial regression was used to predict this outcome. With this type of regression, the likelihood of each outcome (mutual and one-sided IPV victimization) is predicted compared to the reference category (no IPV victimization).

The coefficients and relative risk ratios (RRR) for this model are displayed in Table 6.10. The coefficients and RRRs for mutual IPV victimization are displayed in the left columns, and the model predicting one-sided IPV victimization is displayed in the right columns.

As set forth in Table 6.10, the female partner's Wave One violent offending is a strong, positive, and significant predictor of mutual IPV victimization. Holding all other variables constant, a one unit increase in the female partner's violent offending increases the relative risk of mutual IPV victimization over no IPV victimization by a factor of 64.49 (exp[4.17], p-value < 0.001). Conversely, the female partner's involvement in past violent victimization (non-partner related) significantly decreased the relative risk of mutual IPV victimization compared to no IPV victimization (exp[-9.07] < 0.01, p-value < 0.001). These relationships are consistent with expectations. Couples in which the female partner is more physically developed, has higher self-esteem, and has a hard time getting along with others in school (school trouble) have an increased risk of mutual IPV victimization.

While the female partner's involvement in past violence significantly influences the risk of mutual IPV victimization, the male partner's past violence does not. The male partner's involvement in past violent offending increases the risk of mutual IPV victimization (exp[1.70] = 5.46, p-value > 0.05), and involvement in past violent victimization decreases the risk of mutual IPV victimization (exp[-2.60] = 0.07, p-value > 0.05). However, neither of these coefficients is statistically significant.

Significant male-partner predictors of couple-level mutual IPV victimization include males who come from two-parent homes, have increased parental supervision, experience symptoms of depression, have increased self-esteem, have a hard time getting along with others in school, and who use tobacco. Couples whose male partners come from two-parent homes and have increased levels of parental supervision experience a decrease in the relative risk of mutual IPV victimization (compared to no IPV victimization). Couples whose male partners have increased levels of depressive symptoms, self-esteem, and trouble getting along with others in school experience an increase in relative risk of mutual IPV victimization, holding all other variables constant.

Table 6.10. Multinomial Models Predicting Mutual and One-Sided Couple Violence[a]

	Mutual IPV[b]	One-Sided IPV
	RR Ratio	
Female Partner's Predictors		
Wave One Violent Offending	64.49***	5.99*
Wave One Violent Victimization	<0.01***	0.17**
Drug Use	19.94	0.70
Family SES	5.93	1.78*
Physical Development	25.64*	1.09
Two-Parent Home	0.01	1.71
Drunkenness	1.59	1.23
Parental Supervision	7.15	0.73
Depression	0.20	0.66
Self-Esteem	91.49*	0.90
School Trouble	61.99***	1.47
Male Partner's Predictors		
Wave One Violent Offending	5.46	1.49
Wave One Violent Victimization	0.07	1.16
Drug Use	3.13	2.94*
Family SES	0.85	1.60*
Two-Parent Home	0.05**	1.32
Parental Supervision	0.15*	1.37
Depression	391.69**	4.34
Self-Esteem	692.09***	1.79
School Trouble	22.07*	3.68*
Tobacco Use	1.07	1.05*
Relationship Characteristics		
Relationship Duration	5.39*	1.19
Emotional Intensity	0.28**	0.58***
Sexual Activity	10.04**	2.67***
Constant (Std. Error)	-69.98**	-10.45*
	(19.45	(4.85)

* p<.05, ** p<.01, *** p<.001

a. To save space, certain weak and non-significant coefficients are not displayed, including tobacco use and male partner's physical development and drunkenness.

b. The reference category is no IPV victimization.

The characteristics of these couples also significantly influence the relative risk of mutual IPV victimization. A one-unit increase in the length of the relationship increases the relative risk of mutual IPV victimization over no IPV victimization by a factor of 5.39 (exp[1.68], p-value < 0.05). A one-unit increase in the emotional intensity of the relationship decreases the relative risk of mutual IPV victimization over no IPV victimization by a factor of 0.28 (exp[-1.26], p-value < 0.01), while an increase in the sexual activity in the relationship increases the relative risk of mutual IPV victimization (exp[2.31] = 10.04,p-value < 0.01). Thus, longer and more sexually involved relationships set the stage for mutual IPV, and more affectionate, non-physical activities are associated with a decrease in mutual IPV victimization.

Based on the coefficients and RRRs displayed in the right side of Table 6.10, we observe that the female partner's involvement in past violent offending increases the relative risk of one-sided IPV in the couple over no IPV, and the female's past experience with violent victimization decreases the risk of one-sided IPV. A one-unit increase in the female partner's involvement in past violent offending increases the relative risk of the couple experiencing one-sided IPV over no IPV by nearly six-fold (exp[1.79] = 5.99, p-value < 0.05). An increase in the female partner's reports of past violent victimization decreases the relative risk of one-sided IPV for the couple by a factor of 0.17 (exp[-1.77], p-value < 0.01). Additionally, couples whose female partners come from more affluent homes experience an increase in the relative risk of one-sided IPV over no IPV (exp[0.58] = 1.78, p-value < 0.05).

Just as we observed with the coefficients predicting couple-level mutual IPV, the male partner's involvement in past violence (both offending and victimization) does not significantly influence the couple's relative risk of one-sided IPV. However, the male partner's drug use, family SES, trouble in school, and tobacco use all significantly increase the relative risk of couple-level one-sided IPV over no IPV.

Couple characteristics, including the emotional intensity of the relationship and the amount of sexual activity, significantly influenced the relative risk of one-sided IPV over no IPV. A one-unit increase in the emotional, non-physical activity within the relationship decreased the relative risk of one-sided IPV by a factor of 0.58 (exp[-0.55], p-value < 0.001). Conversely, more sexually active couples experienced an increase in the relative risk of one-sided IPV (exp[0.98] = 2.67, p-value < 0.001). The length of the relationship did not significantly influence the relative risk of one-sided IPV.

Wave Two IPV Victimization and Wave Two Deviant Behavior

In the following analyses, couple-level measures of mutual IPV, one-sided IPV with a female victim, and one-sided IPV with a male victim are used to predict Wave Two individual-level violent offending, violent victimization, delinquency, and drug use. Because these data are nested, HLM models are used in the following analyses. Poisson distributions that take into account the over-dispersion of the dependent variables are used in the analyses predicting Wave Two violent offending, violent victimization, and general delinquency. These models approximate the negative binomial regression models used in Chapter 5 to predict these same outcomes.

Because Wave Two drug use is not continuous, it violates the assumption of most regression techniques that outcome variables are normally distributed. Typically, an HLM model would attempt to predict fitted values across the entire range of given values, which in this case would only be from zero to one. Thus, if this distribution was treated as though it was a product of normally distributed HLM models, the fitted values would almost always be too high or too low. Not correcting for the abnormal distribution would result in residuals that tend to cluster around two points rather than a normal distribution which would cluster around the mean. In order to correct for this distribution a generalized linear model with a Bernoulli distribution at level one is used.

The Level One model (individual-level) is represented by the following equation:

[1] $\text{Logn}[\text{odds}(\text{outcome}_{ij} = 1)] = \beta 0j + \beta 1jX.j + \beta 2jX.j + \ldots$
        $\beta kjX.j$

In this equation, the log odds of Wave Two drug use for adolescent i in relationship j is a function of the k individual-level predictors.

The Level Two model (couple-level) is represented by the following three equations:

[2] $\beta 01 = \gamma 00 + \gamma 01 X1. + \gamma 02 X2. + \gamma 0k Xk. + \mu 0j$
[3] $\beta 1j = \gamma 10 + \mu 1j$
[4] $\beta kj = \gamma k0$

In equation 2, $\beta 01$ is a function of the k individual-level measures centered on their grand mean. The μ terms in equations 2 and 3, are couple-level error terms that represent the unique effect of couple j on variable k, net of the covariates.

In Table 6.11, the HLM models predicting Wave Two violent offending based on couple-level mutual and one-sided IPV are displayed. For both Models 1 and 2, the coefficients are displayed to the left, and the event rate ratios (ERR) are displayed in the right columns. The ERR represents the percent change in the expected count for the outcomes.

In Model 1, Wave One violent offending and violent victimization are not controlled for in the analysis. None of the couple-level measures of IPV victimization are significant or large in size. The only significant couple-level measure in this model is the amount of sexual activity within the relationship. A one-unit increase in the amount of sexual activity within the relationship is associated with a 48% increase in the expected count of Wave Two violent offending (exp[0.39], p-value < 0.01), holding all of the other variables constant.

Based on the individual-level measures in Model 1, being male and being African American are both associated with a significant increase in the expected count of violent offending. An increase in age on the other hand, significantly decreases the expected count of violent offending by 25% (exp[-0.28], p-value < 0.001). Both excessive drinking and depressive symptoms are associated with a significant increase in violent offending.

In Model 2, prior violent offending and violent victimization are controlled for in the analysis. Once again, the amount of sexual activity within the relationship is the only significant predictor of Wave Two individual level violent offending. At the individual-level, as expected, prior violent offending and violent victimization are among the strongest predictors of Wave Two violent offending. Prior violent offending increases the expected count of Wave Two violent offending by 49% (exp[0.40], p-value < 0.001), and prior violent victimization increases the expected count by 58% (exp[0.46], p-value < 0.001). The other individual-level measures that were significant in Model 1 remain significant, with the exception of race (being African American) and age.

Table 6.11. Poisson Models Predicting Wave Two Violent Offending[a]

	Model 1	Model 2
	ER Ratio	
Level-Two Measures		
Mutual IPV	1.65	1.38
One-Sided IPV - Female Victim	1.13	1.10
One-Sided IPV - Male Victim	1.18	0.79
Duration	0.98	0.93
Emotional Intensity	0.92	0.92
Sexual Activity	1.48**	1.40*
Level-One Measures		
Wave One Violent Offending	--	1.49***
Wave One Violent Victimization	--	1.58***
Gender (male)	3.42***	1.90**
African American	2.17**	1.21
Other Race	1.51ʳ	1.17
Physical Development	0.72	0.66*
Two-Parent Home	0.83	0.77
Age (in years)	0.75***	0.84
Family SES	0.92	0.93
Unstructured Socializing	1.08	1.11
Drunkenness	1.22***	1.20**
Tobacco Use	1.01	1.00
Parental Supervision	1.11	1.14
Depression	2.53**	1.96*
Self-Esteem	1.22	1.07
School Trouble	0.99	1.02
Intercept	2.31	0.61

* p<.05, ** p<.01, *** p<.001

a. These models take into account over-dispersion.

Table 6.12. Poisson Models Predicting Wave Two Violent
Victimization[a]

	Model 1	Model 2
	ER Ratio	
Level-Two Measures		
Mutual IPV	1.65	1.31
One-Sided IPV - Female Victim	2.08*	2.11*
One-Sided IPV - Male Victim	1.27	0.90
Duration	1.16	1.12
Emotional Intensity	0.96	0.99
Sexual Activity	0.97	0.90
Level-One Measures		
Wave One Violent Victimization	--	1.28*
Wave One Violent Offending	--	1.69**
Gender (male)	7.29***	4.56***
African American	2.28**	1.57
Other Race	1.40	1.10
Physical Development	0.62	0.61
Two-Parent Home	0.92	0.72
Age (in years)	0.83*	0.94
Family SES	0.90	0.89
Unstructured Socializing	1.38**	1.40**
Drunkenness	0.99	1.02
Tobacco Use	1.03*	1.01
Parental Supervision	0.94	0.95
Depression	2.99**	2.29*
Self-Esteem	1.48	1.24
School Trouble	0.97	0.93
Intercept	0.08	0.03

* $p<.05$, ** $p<.01$, *** $p<.001$

a. These models take into account over-dispersion.

In Table 6.12, couple-level IPV victimization is used to predict
Wave Two violent victimization (non-partner related). Based on Model
1, the only significant couple-level predictor of Wave Two individual-
level violent victimization is one-sided IPV in which the female partner
was the victim. This type of IPV victimization is associated with a

more than 200% increase in the expected count of Wave Two violent victimization (exp[0.73], p-value < 0.05). Neither mutual IPV victimization, nor one-sided IPV victimization with a male victim were significantly associated with the outcome.

At the individual level, being male and being African American were both associated with an increase in the expected count of Wave Two non-partner related violent victimization. Age, on the hand, was associated with a 17% decrease in the expected count of violent victimization (exp[-0.19], p-value < 0.05). The amount of time spent in unstructured socializing, the level of tobacco use, and the amount of depressive symptoms reported by the respondent were all associated with an increase in Wave Two violent victimization.

In Model 2 in Table 6.12, prior violent victimization and violent offending are both controlled for in the analysis. At the couple-level, one-sided IPV victimization with a female victim remains a strong and significant predictor of Wave Two individual-level violent victimization. In fact, the size of this coefficient increases slightly (exp[0.75] = 2.11, p-value < 0.05). None of the other couple-level factors are significant predictors of Wave Two violent victimization.

At the individual level, past violent victimization and violent offending are both significantly associated with an increase in Wave Two violent victimization. Being male, being involved in more unstructured socializing, and being more depressed are also associated with an increase in violent victimization. Race (being African American) and age are no longer significant in the second model.

In Table 6.13, models predicting Wave Two delinquency based on couple-level IPV victimization are displayed. As can be seen in Model 1, both mutual IPV and one-sided IPV with a female victim are associated with an increase in Wave Two individual-level delinquency. Being in a couple that experienced mutual IPV is associated with a 92% increase in the expected count of delinquency (exp[0.65], p-value < 0.01), and being in a couple with one-sided IPV with a female victim is associated with a 61% increase (exp[0.48], p-value < 0.05).

Other significant couple-level characteristics include the emotional intensity and sexuality activity involved in the relationship. A one-unit increase in the amount of non-physical, affectionate activity decreases the expected count of individual-level delinquency by 15% (exp[-0.16], p-value < 0.001). A one-unit increase in the amount of sexual activity within the relationship increases the expected count of individual-level delinquency by 44% (exp[0.37], p-value < 0.05).

Table 6.13. Poisson Models Predicting Wave Two Delinquency[a]

	Model 1	Model 2
	ER Ratio	
Level-Two Measures		
Mutual IPV	1.92**	1.43
One-Sided IPV - Female Victim	1.61*	1.49
One-Sided IPV - Male Victim	1.30	1.01
Duration	0.87	0.84*
Emotional Intensity	0.85*	0.90
Sexual Activity	1.44***	1.25**
Level-One Measures		
Wave One Delinquency	--	1.33***
Gender (male)	1.46**	1.13
African American	1.51	1.75*
Other Race	1.51*	1.35
Physical Development	0.90	1.05
Two-Parent Home	1.18	1.11
Age (in years)	0.77***	0.83**
Family SES	1.17**	1.13*
Unstructured Socializing	0.94	0.97
Drunkenness	1.27***	1.15**
Tobacco Use	1.02***	1.01
Parental Supervision	0.95	1.01
Depression	1.69**	1.46*
Self-Esteem	0.85	0.85
School Trouble	0.91	0.96
Intercept	31.77**	6.64

* p<.05, ** p<.01, *** p<.001
a. These models take into account over-dispersion.

At the individual level, being male is associated with a 46% increase in the expected count of Wave Two delinquency. (exp[0.38], p-value < 0.001), and individuals from other races (i.e., not African American or white) experience a 51% increase (exp[0.41], p-value <

0.05). An increase in age is associated with a decrease in delinquency, while coming from a more affluent home, being involved in excessive alcohol use, an increase in tobacco use, and an increase in depressive symptoms are all associated with a significant increase in delinquency.

In the second model in Table 6.13, controlling for prior delinquency reduces the coefficients for couple-level IPV and one-sided IPV with a female victim in size and renders them non-significant. The emotional intensity within the relationship is also now non-significant, while the coefficient for the amount of sexual activity within the relationship remains significant (exp[0.22] = 1.25, p-value < 0.01). Curiously, the coefficient for the length of the relationship is now significant in the second model. A one-unit increase in the length of the relationship decreases the expected count of delinquency by 16% (exp[-0.18], p-value < 0.05).

At the individual level, a one-unit increase in the amount of prior delinquency increases the expected count of Wave Two delinquency by 33% (exp[0.29], p-value < 0.001). Gender, being from a race described as "other," and tobacco use are no longer significant predictors of Wave Two delinquency in Model 2, whereas being African American becomes significant in this model. Being African American is associated with a 75% increase in the expected count of Wave Two delinquency (exp[0.56], p-value < 0.05). Age, family SES, excessive drinking, and depression remain significant predictors of Wave Two individual-level delinquency in Model 2.

In Table 6.14, models predicting Wave Two drug use based on IPV victimization are displayed. For both Models 1 and 2, the coefficients are displayed in the left columns and the odds ratios are displayed in the right columns. The odds ratios reflect the expected increase in the odds of drug use.

In Model 1, the couple-level measures of IPV are all non-significant. Couple-level IPV does not appear to influence the likelihood of individual drug use in Wave Two. The only significant couple-level measures of Wave Two individual-drug use are the emotional intensity of the relationships and the amount of sexual activity involved in the relationship. A one-unit increase in the emotional intensity of the relationship decreases the odds of individual-level drug use by 31% (exp[-0.37], p-value < 0.05). A one-unit increase in the amount of sexual activity within the relationship increases the odds of individual-level drug use by 66% (exp[0.51], p-value < 0.05).

Table 6.14. Logistic Models Predicting Wave Two Drug Use[a]

	Model 1	Model 2
	Odds Ratio	
Level-Two Measures		
Mutual IPV	2.07	1.72
One-Sided IPV - Female Victim	1.34	1.60
One-Sided IPV - Male Victim	1.93	1.81
Duration	0.99	1.10
Emotional Intensity	0.69*	0.68*
Sexual Activity	1.66*	1.45
Level-One Measures		
Wave One Drug Use	--	6.82***
Gender (male)	1.87**	1.77*
African American	0.94	0.94
Other Race	3.17**	2.72*
Physical Development	0.75	0.68
Two-Parent Home	0.34**	0.35**
Age (in years)	0.73**	0.70**
Family SES	1.24	1.23
Unstructured Socializing	1.25	1.18
Drunkenness	1.94***	1.83***
Tobacco Use	1.05***	1.05***
Parental Supervision	1.24	1.22
Depression	5.03***	5.48***
Self-Esteem	1.39	1.42
School Trouble	0.80	0.68
Intercept	0.43	0.95

* p<.05, ** p<.01, *** p<.001
a. These models take into account over-dispersion.

At the individual level, being male is associated with a significant increase in the odds of drug use (exp[0.63] = 1.87, p-value < 0.001), as is being from the "other" racial category (exp[1.15] = 3.17, p-value < 0.01). Coming from a two-parent home and being older are both associated with a decrease in the expected odds of drug use (exp[-1.09] = 0.34, p-value < 0.01, and exp[-0.32] = 0.73, p-value < 0.01, respectively). Excessive drinking, an increase in tobacco use, and an increase in depressive symptoms are all associated with an increase in the expected odds of Wave Two individual-level drug use. In Model 2 in Table 6.14, the couple-level measure of the emotional intensity of the relationship remains about the same size and is still significant. However, once prior drug use is controlled for the measure for the amount of sexual activity within the relationship is reduced in size and is no longer significant. The other couple-level predictors of Wave Two individual-level drug use remain non-significant.

At the individual level, prior drug use significantly increases the odds of Wave Two drug use by more than six-fold (exp[1.92] = 6.82, p-value < 0.001). The other individual-level measures that were significant in the first model remain significant and similar in size and strength in the second model in Table 6.14.

CONCLUSIONS

The results in this section provide mixed support for the expectation that the risk factors and correlates of IPV victimization will vary based on whether the IPV is experienced by only one or both individuals within the relationship. In the analyses predicting coup-level mutual and one-sided IPV victimization, the female partner's prior violence was a strong, significant, and positive predictor of both types of IPV victimization, whereas the female partner's prior victimization had a negative relationship with these outcomes. The male partner's prior violence was not significantly related to these outcomes. It was hypothesized that prior violent offending would increase the occurrence of mutual IPV victimization, and prior violent victimization would decrease the occurrence of this outcome. This expectation was only partially supported, given the male partner's violence null relationship with this outcome.

It was also hypothesized that prior violent offending would decrease the occurrence of one-sided IPV victimization, while prior violent victimization would increase the occurrence of this outcome, especially for the females. However, this expectation was not met; in fact, the opposite was found to be the case.

In the models predicting Wave Two deviant behaviors based on Wave Two IPV victimization, all types of IPV victimization were not significant factors in most of these analyses, even before controlling for prior behaviors. One of the few expectations includes the models predicting Wave Two individual-level violent victimization. Being in a couple that experienced one-sided IPV, for which the female partner was the victim, was associated with an increase in Wave Two violent victimization even after controlling for prior behaviors.

The one other exception includes the models predicting Wave Two individual-level delinquency. Before controlling for prior delinquency, being involved in a couple that experienced both mutual IPV and one-sided IPV with a female victim were both associated with an increase in Wave Two individual-level delinquency. However, once prior delinquency was controlled for, these significant relationships disappeared. Overall, the results of these analyses provide only minimal support for the expectations explicated at the outset of the study.

In review, in Chapter 4, the question of whether prior violent offending and violent victimization were predictive of subsequent (Wave Two) IPV victimization was addressed. In Chapter 5, the question of whether Wave Two violent offending, violent victimization, general delinquency, and drug use were related to Wave Two IPV victimization, even after controlling for Wave One occurrences of these same behaviors was addressed. Finally, in Chapter 6, the nature of the relationships between IPV victimization (including mutual and one-sided IPV victimization), general violence, general violent victimization, and other deviant behaviors over time was explored. In the final chapter the implications of these findings are discussed.

CHAPTER 7

Towards an Integrated Model of General Violence and Intimate Partner Violence

INTRODUCTION

Although several studies have examined adolescent IPV, all have had serious shortcomings. Most of these studies did not control adequately for prior behaviors or examine both male and female samples. Additionally, none of these prior studies examined the role of friendship networks, or whether the violence in these relationships was mutual or one-sided. The present research examined the influence of prior general violence on the risk of IPV victimization, and whether IPV victimization influenced subsequent deviant behaviors even after controlling for prior behaviors. This research also considered the extent to which general violent behavior and IPV victimization are related, and part of this research included measures of mutual and one-sided IPV victimization. In doing so, this study provided a substantially more complete examination of adolescent IPV.

The results of this study revealed that for adolescents general violence and IPV victimization are not completely separate phenomena; the overlap between victimization and offending that exists in general violence also extends to IPV. A large proportion of individuals who were victimized by their intimate partners also engaged in prior violent offending and were victims of non-partner related violent victimization. In the short-term, IPV victimization is also related to violent offending, non-partner related victimization, delinquency, and drug use, even after controlling for prior instances of these behaviors. Thus, just as general violent offending and violent victimization overlap (i.e., many offenders are also victims and *vice versa*), so do general violence (both offending and victimization) and IPV victimization. A large proportion of adolescent IPV victims are also violent offenders and have also been victimized by general violence. This pattern of overlap suggests that IPV victimization is similar to general violence.

Although there are similarities, IPV victimization and general violence are nonetheless different in two major ways. First, IPV victimization and other deviant behaviors (e.g., violent offending, general delinquency) are not as strongly related as once thought. After controlling for prior behaviors, the strength of the relationship between IPV victimization and same-wave deviant behaviors shrinks; prior deviant behaviors have, by far, the strongest relationships with subsequent deviant behaviors. The weak relationships between IPV victimization and concurrent deviant behaviors reveals a pattern that is not similar to that of general violence. One notable exception to this finding is drug use; the relationship between IPV victimization and same-wave drug use maintained its strength even after controlling for prior drug use.

The second way in which IPV victimization and general violence differ is that there are different types of IPV that vary somewhat in their risk factors and correlates. In this study two main types of IPV were investigated; one was more similar to general violence (mutual IPV victimization), and the other that was different from general violence (one-sided IPV victimization). The results of this study indicate that IPV victimization is both similar and dissimilar to that of general violence. Intimate partner violence victimization shares a reciprocal relationship with general violent behavior, yet certain types of IPV victimization are not as strongly related with general violent behavior. Below, the limitations and strengths, results, and implications of this study are discussed in further detail.

LIMITATIONS AND STRENGTHS OF THIS STUDY

This study provides a comprehensive examination of adolescent IPV. However, this research is limited in two major ways by the data upon which it relies. The first involves the measure of IPV provided by Add Health, which has problems similar to that of the Conflict Tactics Scale (CTS). That is, the respondents were not asked about the contexts of instances of IPV, the motivations of this abuse, or the consequences of this abuse. Also, given the wording of the questions included in the IPV measures, this measure likely captures many less serious instances of IPV. This limitation could explain why males and females had similar rates of IPV victimization.

This study gave us the unique ability to tell whether one or both of the individuals within a couple reported IPV victimization. However, just as the overall measure of IPV victimization lacks context, so does the measure of mutual and one-sided IPV victimization relied upon in Chapter 6. We can tell only whether one or both individuals within a couple reported victimization, but we cannot tell what motivated the violence, whether either or both were injured, who initiated the violence, or who used more force. Additionally, the size of the sample used in Chapter 6 was very small, and it may not be representative of all adolescent romantic relationships. More studies are needed to assess the prevalence of intimate terrorism, situational couple violence, violent resistance, and mutual violent control among adolescents. Additionally, more studies are needed to examine the risk factors and correlates of each type of IPV victimization.

The second major limitation involved the peer network data. Although these data gave this study an advantage in measuring peer network delinquency and violence and other peer network structural characteristics directly from the respondents' peers, these data were somewhat problematic because there was a great deal of missing data. As described in Chapter 3, respondents could be connected to only those peers who were included in the study, and the survey administrators were unable to connect several of the peer nominations. Moreover, the measures of peer network delinquency and violence likely captured many less serious instances of delinquency and abuse (described below). More extensive measures of peer delinquency and violence possibly could have yielded significant results.

Despite these limitations, the research is one of the most complete studies of adolescent IPV to date. The study involved a large, nationally representative sample of adolescents. Questions were posed from both theories of general crime and theories specific to IPV. In addition, the statistical analyses involved advanced multivariate techniques that account for the complex design of Add Health and the nested nature of these data.

SUMMARY OF MAJOR FINDINGS

This research began with five major hypotheses, most of which were at least partially supported by the results. Below, the five hypotheses originally presented in Chapter 2 are re-stated and discussed with respect to the extent to which they were supported by the results.

Hypothesis 1: Prior Violent Offending and Violent Victimization

First, it was hypothesized that prior violent offending and violent victimization would all positively influence the risk of IPV victimization. This hypothesis was based on the premise that early violent offending and violent victimization leave adolescents more vulnerable to entering into abusive relationships. Based on opportunity theories, particularly lifestyle exposure theory, it was argued that individuals who engage in violent behaviors make more attractive victims and they are more likely to engage in behaviors that provoke victimization (e.g., Hindelang et al., 1978; Lauritsen et al., 1991; Sampson and Lauritsen 1990). Also, engaging in criminal and delinquent behaviors leaves deviant adolescents more exposed to deviant others, and this exposure in turn can increase the risk of victimization. This exposure may also increase the likelihood that an individual will select a deviant romantic partner because he or she is more likely to select a mate from the people he or she is around the most (Simons et al., 1993). Finally, based on the general violence literature, there is consistency in victimization over time (Schreck et al. 2006; Wittebrood and Nieuwbeerta 2000). That is, prior victimization is highly predictive of subsequent victimization. A small proportion of victims usually account for a disproportionate number of victimizations.

The results of this research support this hypothesis linking IPV and prior violent offending and prior violent victimization. Prior violent offending and violent victimization both increased the odds of IPV victimization, although violent victimization was a slightly stronger predictor of IPV victimization. These results were consistent for both verbal and physical IPV victimization.

Also in line with opportunity theories, unstructured socializing (i.e., time spent "just hanging out") increased the odds of IPV victimization. Thus, it appears that adolescents who spend more time hanging out with their peers in the absence of responsible adults and who spend less time in, say, athletic activities, are more likely to be victimized.

Depression was, by far, the strongest predictor of IPV victimization; adolescents indicating problems with depression were also more likely to become victims of IPV. However, the direction of this relationship is unclear. That is, does depression increase the likelihood of IPV victimization, does IPV victimization lead to depression, or is this relationship reciprocal? Because Add Health did not include a Wave One measure of IPV victimization, this relationship cannot be further examined in the present study. Several studies have linked IPV victimization to depression and poor mental health (e.g., Campbell 2002; Coker et al. 2002), but these studies did not control for pre-existing levels of depression. Thus, the question of causality is still an open one requiring further research.

Hypothesis 2: Effects of IPV Victimization

The second major hypothesis of this research was that IPV victimization would positively increase the likelihood of violent offending, non-partner related violent victimization, general delinquency, and drug use, even after controlling for prior instances of these same behaviors. This hypothesis was based on research that has linked IPV victimization with a variety of antisocial behaviors among adolescents (e.g., Ackard et al. 2007; Roberts et al. 2003), as well as research that has linked non-relationship victimization to offending (e.g., Macmillan 2001; Menard 2002). Just as offending and victimization predict one another (Shaffer and Ruback 2002), IPV victimization should have a similar relationship with deviant outcomes and subsequent victimization.

This hypothesis was also supported by the results. Abuse by an intimate partner was positively and significantly related to all four outcomes, even after controlling for prior instances of these behaviors. Several studies have linked IPV victimization to a variety of deviant outcomes (e.g., Eaton et al. 2007; Silverman et al. 2001), although, many of these studies did not control for prior instances of these same behaviors. Even though prior deviant behaviors are highly predictive of future deviant behaviors, IPV victimization is also associated with short-term deviant behaviors. Moreover, the research reported in this monograph suggests the relationships between IPV victimization and deviant behaviors over time are not spurious.

For models predicting violent victimization and violent offending based on IPV victimization, controlling for prior violence significantly reduced the effect of IPV victimization, but it remained positive and significant. An interaction term between prior violent offending and IPV victimization revealed that IPV victims who also engaged in prior violent offending were less likely to engage in subsequent violence. Similarly, an interaction term between prior non-partner related violent victimization and IPV victimization revealed that responders who were previously victimized and who were victims of IPV at Wave Two were less likely to be victimized by general violence at Wave Two. For both of these models (predicting violent offending and violent victimization), the main effects for IPV victimization increased after adding the interaction terms. Thus, respondents with a history of violent offending and violent victimization do not appear to engage in more of each (offending and victimization) as a result of IPV victimization. That is, IPV victimization increases violent offending and violent victimization only for those respondents who did not previously engage in violent offending and who were not previously the victims of general violence. This pattern, if true, suggests that IPV may be an entry point to more general violence.

In the models predicting delinquency, controlling for prior delinquency did not decrease the effect of IPV victimization, although prior delinquency was a much stronger predictor of subsequent delinquency than was IPV victimization. After an interaction term was added between prior delinquency and IPV victimization, the main effect for IPV victimization increased in size. Similar to the models predicting Wave Two violent offending and violent victimization, the effect of the interaction term revealed that adolescents who engaged in prior delinquency and who were victims of IPV at Wave Two engaged in less delinquency. Again, being victimized by an intimate partner appears to increase deviant behavior only for those adolescents who did not engage in prior deviant behavior.

In models predicting Wave Two drug use based on IPV victimization, controlling for prior drug use decreased the effect of IPV victimization only slightly. Even after controlling for prior use, IPV victimization significantly increased the odds of within-wave drug use. Unlike the previous models, there were no significant interactions. Thus, IPV victimization appears to increase drug use net of prior drug use.

Hypothesis 3: IPV and Peer Network Characteristics
The third hypothesis predicted that peer network characteristics would influence the likelihood of IPV victimization and the deviant behaviors associated with IPV victimization. This hypothesis was not supported. It was predicted that less popular adolescents would have fewer peers to recognize abusive behavior and intervene in these relationships. However, both popular and less popular respondents were vulnerable to IPV victimization. It was also predicted that respondents with more deviant peers would be more likely to become victims of IPV, which did not turn out to be the case. All of the peer network characteristics had only weak and non-significant effects on the likelihood of IPV victimization.

In the models predicting violent offending, violent victimization, delinquency and drug use, all of the peer network characteristics included in the model were weak and non-significant. They did not interact with any of the other measures, including IPV victimization. Adolescents with more delinquent and violent friends did not engage in more of these deviant behaviors in response to IPV victimization.

Given that prior research has established the strong influence of peers on deviant behavior (e.g., Haynie 2002), it is surprising that none of these measures was significant in predicting these deviant outcomes. However, there is a reasonable explanation for the difference in the effects of peer network characteristics between this study and other studies. The measure of peer network delinquency used here captures only very minor deviance, whereas other studies have used measures of more serious delinquency and violence.

For example, in Haynie's (2002) study of delinquent friendship networks and individual offending, Haynie used the saturation sample from Add Health. In the saturation sample, all enrolled students from 12 different schools were selected for in-home interviews. Thus, all of these students (approximately 2,600) were asked more detailed questions about their delinquency and violent offending, compared to students who were given only the in-school questionnaire. The in-home questionnaire included more serious measures of delinquency and violent offending compared to the in-school questionnaire. The peer network delinquency and violence measures used in this study are based on questions from the in-school questionnaire. If this study had used data from only the saturation sample, it could have included more serious measures of peer network delinquency, and the results of this study may well have been different. However, using this type of measure would have greatly limited the sample size for investigating the correlates and consequences of IPV.

Hypothesis 4: Differences by Gender

The fourth hypothesis set forth at the outset of this study predicted that the relationship between deviant behavior and IPV victimization would be different for male and female victims. This hypothesis was based on the fact that gender plays an important role in predicting general violence and some types of IPV victimization. Also, past research has shown that males and females sometimes differ in their pathways to offending. Further, some research has shown that female offenders may be more vulnerable to partner violence victimization, and that oftentimes deviant behavior among women is a result of IPV victimization.

This hypothesis found mixed results in this study. Some differences between males and females were found, but not many. In models predicting IPV victimization, violent offending and childhood maltreatment were much stronger predictors of IPV victimization for males than for females. Males who engaged in violent offending and who were victimized by their parents as children were more likely than were similarly situated females to also enter into abusive relationships.

Also, prior non-partner-related violent victimization was a stronger predictor of IPV victimization for females than for males in the Add Health data, but the difference between these two groups was not statistically significant.

It was also expected that the proportion of opposite sex friends in the respondent's peer network would affect the likelihood of IPV victimization, and that this effect would be positive for females and negative for males. That is, having more opposite sex friends should increase the likelihood of IPV victimization for females and decrease the likelihood of IPV victimization for males. Contrary to this expectation, this measure was not significant for either males or females, and the effect did not go in opposite directions for these two groups.

In models predicting Wave Two violent offending and violent victimization, prior violent victimization was a significantly larger predictor of both outcomes for females compared to males. Compared to males, females who had been the victims of prior general violence engaged in more violent offenses and were the victims of more violent offenses. That prior violent victimization was a stronger predictor of these outcomes for females than for males is consistent with expectations. Past research indicates that there is a strong relationship between victimization and offending for females (for a review, see Zahn et al. 2010). For example, Chesney-Lind (1997) has written extensively about the prevalence of past victimization among female offenders, including incarcerated females. Also, Miller's (1998, 2001) studies of male and female gang members have revealed that past victimization is somewhat more common among female gang members compared to their male counterparts. More female gang members report abusive home environments, and once these females join gangs they are more vulnerable to subsequent victimization (including IPV victimization).

It was expected that IPV victimization would be a stronger predictor of violent offending and delinquency for males than for females. However, the effect of IPV victimization was not statistically different for males and females. It was also expected that females would be more likely than males to use drugs in response to IPV victimization. However, the effect of IPV victimization on drug use did not differ significantly for males and females in the Add Health data.

That there were few differences between males and females in the causes and correlates of adolescent IPV victimization is contrary to the study's original expectations. However, the lack of differences in these findings is consistent with other lines of research on the absence of male-female differences, including research on cognitive abilities (Feingold 1988) and interpersonal communication (Canary and Dindia 2006). Also, although the differences between males and females in delinquency have been highlighted throughout this research, there are also many ways that males and females are similar in regards to delinquency. After reviewing several studies of adolescent delinquency, Zahn et al. (2010) concluded that economic disadvantage, early exposure to violence, childhood maltreatment, and limited parental supervision were all associated with an increase in delinquency for both males and females.

Hypothesis 5: One-Sided vs. Mutual IPV Victimization

In the final hypothesis it was predicted that both the risk factors for IPV victimization and the deviant behaviors associated with IPV victimization would vary depending on whether the partner violence was one-sided or mutual. There were reports of mutual IPV and one-sided IPV victimization in the data, and there were some differences in the predictors and correlates of these different types of IPV victimization as expected.

Prior violent offending should be more predictive than prior violent victimization of mutual IPV victimization. Adolescents who engage in violent offending probably have more violent tendencies and should be more likely to become involved in conflict-ridden relationships. They should be more likely to both perpetrate IPV and be the victims of IPV. Conversely, prior violent victimization should be more predictive of one-sided couple violence compared to prior violent offending. Adolescents who have been the victims of violence in the past should be more prone to future victimization, including IPV victimization.

Consistent with these expectations, the results revealed that the female partner's involvement in prior violent offending was one of the largest predictors of mutual IPV victimization, increasing the risk of mutual IPV victimization for couples over no IPV victimization. Also, consistent with prior expectations, the female partner's past violent victimization greatly decreased the likelihood of mutual IPV victimization for women. In contrast, the male partner's reports of prior general violence (both offending and victimization) did not significantly influence the couple's risk of mutual IPV.

Contrary to what was expected, the female partner's involvement in prior violent offending increased the risk of one-sided IPV victimization within couples, while the female partner's reports of prior violent victimization decreased this risk. Similar to coefficients predicting mutual IPV, the male partner's reports of prior violence did not significantly influence one-sided IPV victimization within couples.

In models predicting mutual and one-sided IPV, it was also expected that mutual and one-sided IPV would have different risk factors, and the results observed were consistent with this expectation. For example, the level of physical development of the female partner increased the risk of mutual IPV over no IPV within couples, but this measure did not increase the risk of one-sided IPV. The same was true for the male partner's level of depressive symptoms and self-esteem, both of which increased the risk of mutual IPV for couples, but not one-sided IP. Conversely, both the male partner's drug use and family's SES increased the risk of one-sided IPV for couples, but did not have a significant effect on mutual IPV. Relationship characteristics, including both the emotional intensity and the amount of sexual activity within the relationship, significantly influenced the risk of mutual and one-sided IPV. Although the length of the relationship did not have a significant relationship with one-sided IPV, it significantly increased the likelihood of mutual IPV.

This study expects to find that adolescents who were victimized by one-sided IPV would be more likely to be under close surveillance and that their behaviors would be micro-managed, just as victims of intimate terrorism (Johnson 2008) or coercive control (Stark 2007) are. This type of abuse should leave adolescents less able to engage in violent offending and delinquency, but would make them more likely to engage in self-destructive behaviors (i.e., drug use) and become victims again (general violent victimization). Victims of mutual IPV, on the other hand, have a history of violent offending, and should therefore be expected to engage in more violent offending in response to IPV victimization compared to victims of one-sided IPV.

The above expectations were partially supported by the results of this study. In models predicting Wave Two violent offending and drug use based on mutual and one-sided IPV victimization, none of the measures of IPV significantly influenced this outcome. One-sided IPV victimization, in which the female partner was victimized, significantly increased Wave Two violent victimization even after controlling for prior general violence (both offending and victimization). This finding was consistent with the expectations described above. Couple-level mutual IPV had a positive and significant relationship with delinquency, which was expected. However, one-sided IPV also had a positive and significant relationship with delinquency. Both of these relationships were no longer significant after controlling for prior delinquency.

Overall, the effects of prior violence on the risk of mutual IPV were consistent with expectations, but the effects of prior violence on one-sided IPV were not. Only one of the expected correlates of these two types of IPV victimization was consistent with expectations (Wave Two violent victimization). General violence was associated with IPV victimization, both in terms of being a risk factor and correlate of mutual and one-sided IPV victimization. However, Wave Two violent offending, delinquency, and drug use did not have the expected relationship with IPV victimization; victims of mutual IPV were not more prone either either to more violent offending or delinquency, and victims of one-sided IPV did not engage in more self-destructive behaviors (i.e., drug use).

It is important to view these findings with some skepticism, however, because the data set was small and the measures of mutual and one-sided IPV were rather crude. More studies are clearly needed to assess the prevalence, risk factors, and correlates of each type of IPV victimization not mediated by depression.

IMPLICATIONS FOR THEORY AND RESEARCH ON IPV

The results of this research have four major implications for theory and research on IPV victimization and general violence. First, the results of this study show that both adolescent males and females are at similar risk for IPV victimization, at least as measured by questions analogous to the CTS. Most theory and research on adolescent IVP victimization is directed towards females, but the results of this study suggest that rates of IPV victimization are similar between both sexes and there are not as many gender differences in the risk factors and correlates of IPV victimization as might be expected. However, it is important to keep in mind that this study included both serious and less serious instances of IPV victimization. Adolescent females are likely more vulnerable to the most serious and injurious forms of IPV victimization. Females are more likely to be injured as a result of IPV victimization (Straus 1997) and they tend to endure more long-term health consequences (Ackard et al. 2007). Had this study included more precise measures of IPV victimization (e.g., the seriousness of the abuse, injuries associated with the abuse), the results may have been different.

Second, the results reported in Chapter 6 revealed that there are multiple types of IPV victimization among adolescents, and these different types of IPV victimization had different predictors and correlates. Thus, we cannot assume that all forms of IPV victimization are the same. Some forms of IPV victimization are probably not as similar to general violent victimization (i.e., one-sided IPV or intimate terrorism) as others (i.e., mutual IPV victimization or situational couple violence). Thus, IPV victimization is not a unique brand of violent victimization that is totally separate from general violence, as some scholars would argue (e.g., DeKeseredy and Kelly 1993; Dobash and Dobash 1979; Dutton 1988). However, Felson's (2002) assumption that "violence is violence" requires some caveats that should be considered when studying IPV victimization. That is, there are multiple types of IPV victimization, some of which are more similar to general violence and some of which are different from general violence.

The third major implication of this study is that IPV victimization, violent offending, and non-partner-related violent victimization do overlap. Opportunity theories are not typically used to explain IPV victimization, but according to the results of this study lifestyle exposure theory can at least partially explain IPV victimization, especially mutual IPV victimization. In this study, the risk of IPV victimization was related to exposure to risk, including the respondents' offending behaviors. The number of delinquent and violent peers in the respondents' social networks (who also represent exposure to risk), on the other hand, did not influence the risk of IPV victimization.

The results of this study suggest that state dependence or population heterogeneity explanations, which are commonly applied to the consistency in victimization over time (Lauritsen and Quinet 1995; Osborn and Tseloni 1998), might be useful for understanding IPV victimization. The state dependence explanation of repeat victimization posits that victimization alters unmeasured aspects of an individual's behavior or lifestyle, which in turn increases the risk of future victimization. In this study, prior violent victimization (not related to partner violence) may alter the individual's psychological well-being or behavior in a way which affects the likelihood that the individual will enter into an abusive relationship. The population heterogeneity explanation of repeat victimization posits that certain individuals are predisposed to victimization (e.g., Hodges and Perry 1999; Lauritsen and Quinet 1999; Wittebrood and Nieuwbeerta 2000). The characteristics that predispose certain individuals to victimization have not been identified at this point.

More studies with more data on psychological well-being are needed to examine whether these explanations are applicable to IPV victimization. With more complete data, we could measure whether prior victimization not only increases depression and reduces self-esteem (as we can with Add Health), but also affects other factors such as anxiety or self-efficacy, for example.

The final major implication of this study for research and theory is that the correlates of IPV victimization are not as strong as previously thought, and the effect of IPV victimization is not the same for all victims. Past studies have shown that IPV victimization is associated with several deviant behaviors, including drug use and delinquency. This study suggests that, although IPV victimization is related to these outcomes, the strength and direction of these relationships are different than previously thought. That is, after controlling for prior deviant behaviors, the relationship between IPV victimization and deviance shrinks. Also, the adolescents' experiences with prior deviant behaviors (i.e., violent offending, violent victimization, and delinquency) moderate the relationship between IPV victimization and these behaviors.

IMPLICATIONS FOR POLICY AND PREVENTION EFFORTS

Teen dating violence has been recognized as a national health problem, and the results of this project have implications for prevention policy in two ways. First, this research has identified additional risk factors of teen dating violence. In particular, this study has shown that early violent behaviors increase the risk of IPV victimization for adolescents. Already "at risk" youth appear to have an increased risk of victimization. Prevention efforts should continue to be directed at all adolescents, but perhaps additional targeted efforts are needed for youth who are already involved in deviant behaviors.

Second, just as there are multiple types of adult IPV, there are multiple types of adolescent IPV. As Johnson (2010) and Johnson and Ferraro (2000) have argued, it is important to make distinctions between different types of IPV, both for the sake of research and theory and for prevention. The results of this study done with the Add Health data suggest that different types of IPV victimization have different origins and correlates. Thus, different strategies are likely required to prevent and intervene in each type of IPV.

With regard to adult IPV, Mills (2003) has argued that police departments have mistakenly adopted singular tactics to deal with IPV. Strategies such as dual arrests or restorative justice are not suited for all types of IPV (e.g., situational couple violence, intimate terrorism). For example, restorative justice may be an appropriate solution to some instances of situational couple violence, but not to intimate terrorism. The same is probably true for adolescent IPV. In the event of mutual IPV victimization, an intervention that involves conflict resolution tactics training or anger management for both parties might be appropriate. Conversely, for one-sided IPV only the aggressor should receive anger management or more punitive measures, while the victim should receive treatment and protection from his or her abuser.

CONCLUSION

Given that most adolescents are involved in romantic relationships and that some of these relationships involve violence, it is important for researchers to investigate the factors that lead to violence and to attempt to understand them in terms of theories of general crime and theories of interpersonal violence. This study used a large, nationally representative sample from the Add Health data in an attempt to meet those goals. More research along these lines is indicated and it is hoped that the findings reported in this study will both inform and stimulate such important and timely work.

References

Ackard, Diann M., Marla E. Eisenberg, and Dianne Neumark-Sztainer. 2007. "Long-Term Impact of Adolescent Dating Violence on the Behavioral and Psychological Health of Male and Female Youth." *The Journal of Pediatrics* 151:476-481.

Acock, Alan C. 2005. "Working with Missing Values." *Journal of Marriage and Family* 67:1012-1028.

Adelman, Madelaine and Sang H. Kil. 2007. "Dating Conflicts: Rethinking Dating Violence and Youth Conflict." *Violence against Women* 13(12):1296-1318.

Agnew, Robert. 1991. "The Interactive Effect of Peer Variables on Delinquency." *Criminology* 29:47-72.

Agnew, Robert. 1992. "Foundations for a General Strain Theory of Crime and Delinquency." *Criminology* 30:47-87.

Agresti, Alan and Barbara Finlay. 1997. *Statistical Methods for the Social Sciences.* Upper Saddle River, NJ: Prentice-Hall.

Akers, Ronald L. 1985. *Deviant Behavior: A Social Learning Approach.* Belmont, CA: Wadsworth Publishing Company.

Akers, Ronald L. Marvin D. Krohn, Lonn Lanza-Kaduce, and Marcia Radosvich. 1979. "Social Learning and Deviant Behavior: A Specific Test of a General Theory." *American Sociological Review* 44:636-655.

Archer, John. 2000. "Sex Differences in Aggression between Heterosexual Partners: A Meta-Analytic Review." *Psychological Bulletin* 126:651-680.

Archer, John. 2006. "Cross-Cultural Differences in Physical Aggression Between Partners: A Social-Role Analysis." *Personality and Social Psychology Review* 10:133-153.

Bachman, Ronet and Linda E. Saltzman. 1995. *Violence against Women: Estimates from the Redesigned Survey.* Special Report.

Washington, D.C.: U.S. Department of Justice, Office of Justice Programs, Bureau of Justice Statistics.

Bergman, Libby. 1992. "Dating Violence among High School Students." *Social Work* 37:21-27.

Beyers, Jennifer M. and Rolf Loeber. 2003. "Untangling Developmental Relations between Depressed Mood and Delinquency in Male Adolescents." *Journal of Abnormal Child Psychology* 31(3):247-266.

Bowker, Lee H., Meda Chesney-Lind, and Joy Pollock. 1978. *Women, Crime, and the Criminal Justice System.* Lexington, MA: Lexington Books.

Briere, John and Marsha Runtz. 1988. "Symptomology Associated with Childhood Sexual Victimization in a Non-Clinical Sample." *Child Abuse Neglect* 12:51-59.

Broidy, Lisa and Robert Agnew. 1997. "Gender and Crime: A General Strain Theory Perspective." *Journal of Research in Crime and Delinquency* 34(3):275-306.

Brown, B. Bradford. 1982. "The Extent and Effects of Peer Pressure among High School Students." *Journal of Youth and Adolescents* 11:121-133.

Bureau of Justice Statistics. 2008. *Crime and Victim Statistics. Washington, D.C.*: U.S. Department of Justice, Office of Justice Programs, Bureau of Justice Statistics. Retrieved March 10, 2009. (http://www.ojp.usdoj.gov/bjs/cvict.htm).

Burgess, Robert L. and Ronald L. Akers. 1966. "A Differential Association-Reinforcement Theory of Criminal Behavior." *Social Problems* 14(2):128-147.

Burnam, Audrey M., Judith A. Stein, Jacqueline M. Golding, Judith M. Siegel, Susan B. Sorenson, Alan B. Forsythe, and Cynthia A. Telles. 1988. "Sexual Assault and Mental Disorders in a Community Population." *Journal of Consulting and Clinical Psychology* 56:843-850.

Busby, Dean M., Thomas B. Holman, and Eric Walker. 2008. "Pathways to Relationship Aggression between Adult Partners." *Family Relations* 57: 72-83.

Byles, Jack A. 1978. "Family Violence: Some Facts and Gaps. A Statistical Overview." Pp. 53-83 in *Domestic Violence: Issues and Dynamic*, edited by Vincent D'Oyley. Toronto: The Ontario Institute for Studies in Education.

Campbell, Jacquelyn C. 2002. "Health Consequences of Intimate Partner Violence." *The Lancet* 359:1331-1336.

Canary, Daniel J. and Kathryn Dindia. 2006. *Sex Differences and Similarities in Communication, Second Edition.* Mahwah, NJ:Lawrence Erlbaum.

Capaldi, Deborah M., Hyoun K. Kim, and Joann W. Shortt. 2007. "Observed Initiation and Reciprocity of Physical Aggression in Young, At-Risk Couples." *Journal of Family Violence* 22:101-111.

Carver, Karen, Kara Joyner, and J. Richard Udry. 2003. "National Estimates of Adolescent Romantic Relationships." Pp. 23-56 in *Adolescent Romantic Relations and Sexual Behavior: Theory, Research and Practical Implications*, edited by Paul Florsheim. Mahwah, NJ: Erlbaum.

Caspi, Avshalom and Terrie E. Moffitt. 1991. "Individual Differences are Accentuated during Periods of Social Change: The Sample Case of Girls at Puberty." *Journal of Personality and Social Psychology* 61:157–168.

Catalano, Shannan M. 2006. *Criminal Victimization, 2005.* Bulletin. Washington, D.C.: U.S. Department of Justice, Office of Justice Programs, Bureau of Justice Statistics.

Chesney-Lind, Meda. 1997. *The Female Offender: Girls, Women, and Crime.* Thousand Oaks, CA: Sage Publications.

Chu, James A. and Diana L. Dill. 1990. "Dissociative Symptoms in Relation to Childhood Physical and Sexual Abuse." *American Journal of Psychiatry* 147:887-892.

Clogg, Clifford C., Eva Petkova, and Adamantios Haritou. 1995. "Statistical Methods for Comparing Regression Coefficients between Models." *American Journal of Sociology* 100:1261-1293.

Cloward, Richard A. and Lloyd Ohlin. 1960. *Delinquency and Opportunity: A Theory of Delinquent Gangs.* New York, NY: The Free Press.

Cohen, Albert K. 1955. *Delinquent Boys: The Culture of the Gang.* New York, NY: The Free Press.

Cohen, Jacob. 1988. *Statistical Power Analysis for the Behavioral Sciences.* Hillsdale, NJ: Lawrence Earlbaum Associates.

Cohen, Lawrence E. and Marcus Felson. 1979. "Social Change and Crime Rate Trends: A Routine Activity Approach." *American Sociological Review* 43:93-109.

Coker, Ann L., Keith E. Davis, Ileana Arias, Sujata Desai, Maureen Sanderson, Heather M. Brandt, and Paige H. Smith. 2002. "Physical and Mental Health Effects of Intimate Partner Violence for Men and Women." *American Journal of Preventative Medicine* 23(4):260-268.

Coker, Ann L., Paige H. Smith, Lesa Bethea, Melissa R. King, and Robert E. McKeown. 2000. "Physical Health Consequences of Physical and Psychological Intimate Partner Violence." *Archives of Family Medicine* 9:451-457.

Collins, W. Andrew. 2003. "More Than a Myth: The Developmental Significance of Romantic Relationships during Adolescence." *Journal of Research on Adolescence* 13(1):1-24.

Connolly, Jennifer, Debra Pepler, Wendy Craig, and Ali Taradash. 2000. "Dating Experiences of Bullies in Early Adolescence." *Child Maltreatment* 5(4):299-310.

Cook, Thomas D. and Donald T. Campbell. 1979. *Quasi-Experimentation, Design and Analysis Issues for Field Settings.* Chicago, IL: Rand McNally College Publishing Co.

Cougle, Jesse R., Heidi Resnick, and Dean G. Kilpatrick. 2009. "A prospective examination of PTSD symptoms as risk factors for subsequent exposure to potentially traumatic events among women." *Journal of Abnormal Psychology* 118:405-411.

Daly, Kathleen and Meda Chesney-Lind. 1988. "Feminism and Criminology." *Justice Quarterly* 5(4):497-538.

Dawson, John M. and Patrick A. Langan. 1994. *Murder in Families.* Special Report. Washington, D.C.: U.S. Department of Justice, Office of Justice Programs, Bureau of Justice Statistics.

DeKeseredy, Walter S. and Katharine Kelly. 1993. "Woman Abuse in University and College Dating Relationships: The Contribution of the Ideology of Familial Patriarchy." *Critical Criminology* 4(2):25-52.

DeKeseredy, Walter S. and Martin D. Schwartz. 1997. "Male Peer Support and Woman Abuse in Postsecondary School Courtship: Suggestions for New Directions in Sociological Research." Pp. 83-96 in *Issues in Intimate Violence,* edited by Raquel Kennedy Bergen. Thousand Oaks, CA: Sage.

DeKeseredy, Walter S., Martin D. Schwartz, Danielle Fagen, and Mandy Hall. 2006. "Separation/Divorce Sexual Assault: The Contribution of Male Support." *Feminist Criminology* 1:228-250.

Demuth, Stephen. 2004. "Understanding the Delinquency and Social Relationships of Loners." *Youth & Society* 35(3):366-392.

Dobash, R. Emerson and Russell Dobash. 1992. *Women, Violence, and Social Change.* New York: Routledge.

Dobash, R. Emerson and Russell Dobash. 1979. *Violence against Wives: A Case against the Patriarchy.* New York: Free Press.

Dobash, Russell P., R. Emerson Dobash, Margo Wilson, and Martin Daly. 1992. "The Myth of Sexual Symmetry in Marital Violence." *Social Problems* 39:71-91.

Duncan, Renae D., Benjamin E. Saunders, Dean G. Kilpatrick, Rochelle F. Hanson, and Heidi S. Resnick. 1996. "Childhood Physical Assault as a Risk Factor for PTSD, Depression and Substance Abuse: Findings from a National Survey." *American Journal of Orthopsychiatry* 66:437-448.

Dutton, Donald G. 1988. *The Domestic Assault of Women: Psychological and Criminal Justice Perspectives.* Boston, MA: Allyn and Bacon.

Eaton, Danice K., Kristen S. Davis, Lisa Barrios, Nancy D. Brener, and Rita K. Noonan. 2007. "Associations of Dating Violence with Lifetime Participation, Co-Occurrence, and Early Initiation of Risk Behaviors among U.S. High School Students." *Journal of Interpersonal Violence* 22(5):586-602.

Fagan, Jeffrey, Elizabeth S. Piper, and Yu-The Cheng. 1987. "Contributions of Victimization to Delinquency in Inner Cities." *The Journal of Criminal Law & Criminology* 78(3):586-613.

Feingold, Alan. 1988. "Cognitive Gender Differences are Disappearing." *American Psychologist* 43(2):95-103.

Feitel, Barbara, Neil Margetson, John Chamas, and Cindy Lipman. 1992. "Psychosocial Background and Behavioral and Emotional Disorders of Homeless and Runaway Youth." *Hospital and Community Psychiatry* 43(2):155–159.

Felson, Marcus. 1998. *Crime and Everyday Life.* Thousand Oaks, CA: Pine Forge.

Felson, Richard B. 1996. "Big people hit little people: Sex differences in physical power and interpersonal violence." *Criminology* 34:433–452.

Felson, Richard B. 2002. *Violence and Gender Reexamined.* Washington, DC: American Psychological Association.

Felson, Richard B. 2006. "Is Violence against Women about Women or about Violence?" *Contexts* 5:21-25.

Felson, Richard B. and Kelsea Jo Lane. 2010. "Does Violence Involving Women and Intimate Partners have a Special Etiology?" *Criminology* 48(1):321-338.

Fiebert, Martin S. 1997. "References Examining Assaults by Women on their Spouses or Male Partners: An Annotated Bibliography." *Sexuality and Culture* 1:273-286.

Forde, David and Leslie Kennedy. 1997. "Risky Lifestyles, Routine Activities, and the General Theory of Crime." *Justice Quarterly* 14:264-294.

Fox, James Alan and Marianne W. Zawitz. 2010. *Homicide Trends in the United States.* Special Report. Washington, D.C.: U.S. Department of Justice, Office of Justice Programs, Bureau of Justice Statistics.

Giordano, Peggy C. 2007. "Recent Research on Gender and Adolescent Relationships: Implications for Teen Dating Violence Research/ Prevention," presentation at the U.S. Departments of Health and Human Services and Justice Workshop on Teen Dating Violence: Developing a Research Agenda to Meet Practice Needs, Crystal City, Va., December 4, 2007.

Giordano, Peggy C., Stephen A. Cernkovich, and M.D. Pugh. 1986. "Friendships and Delinquency." *American Journal of Sociology* 91:1170-1202.

Goodwin, Sandra N., Daniel Chandler, and Joan Meisel. 2003. *Violence against Women: The Role of Welfare Reform.* Research Report. Washington, D.C.: U.S. Department of Justice, Office of Justice Programs, National Institute of Justice.

Gottfredson, Michael R. 1981. "On the Etiology of Criminal Victimization." *Journal of Criminal Law and Criminology* 72:714-726.

Graham-Kevan, Nicola and John Archer. 2005. "Investigating Three Explanations of Women's Relationship Aggression." *Psychology of Women Quarterly* 29(3):270-277.

Gray, Heather M. and Vangie Foshee. 1997. "Adolescent Dating Violence." *Journal of Interpersonal Violence* 12:126-141.

Grogan-Kaylor, Andrew and Melanie D. Otis. 2003. "The Effect of Childhood Maltreatment on Adult Criminality: A Tobit Regression Analysis." *Child Maltreatment* 8(2):129-137.

Halpern, Carolyn T., Selene G. Oslak, Mary L. Young, Sandra L. Martin, and Lawrence L. Kupper. 2001. "Partner Violence among Adolescents in Opposite-Sex Romantic Relationships: Findings from the National Longitudinal Study of Adolescent Health." *American Journal of Public Health* 91(10):1679-1685.

Haynie, Dana L. 2001. "Delinquent Peers Revisited: Does Network Structure Matter?" *American Journal of Sociology* 106:1013-1057.

Haynie, Dana L. 2002. "Friendships Networks and Delinquency: The Relative Nature of Peer Delinquency." *Journal of Quantitative Criminology* 18(2):99-132.

Haynie, Dana L., Darrell Steffensmeier, and Kerryn E. Bell. 2007. "Gender and Serious Violence: Untangling the Role of Friendship Sex Composition and Peer Violence." *Youth Violence and Juvenile Justice* 5:235-253.

Haynie, Dana L., Peggy C. Giordano, Wendy D. Manning, and Monica A. Longmore. 2005. "Adolescent Romantic Relationships and Delinquency Involvement." *Criminology* 43:177-210.

Heitjan, Daniel F. and Srabashi Basu. 1996. "Distinguishing 'Missing at Random' and 'Missing Completely at Random.'" *The American Statistician* 50:207-213.

Hindelang, Michael J. 1976. *Criminal Victimization in Eight American Cities: A Descriptive Analysis of Common Theft and Assault.* Cambridge, MA: Ballinger Publishing Co.

Hindelang, Michael J., Michael R. Gottfredson, and James Garofalo. 1978. *Victims of Personal Crime: An Empirical Foundation for a Theory of Personal Victimization.* Cambridge, MA: Ballinger.

Hodges, Ernest V. and David G. Perry. 1999. "Personal and Interpersonal Antecedents and Consequences of Victimization by Peers." *Journal of Personality and Social Psychology* 76(4):677-685.

Jensen, Gary F. and David Brownfield. 1986. "Gender, Lifestyles, and Victimization: Beyond Routine Activity Theory." *Violence and Victims* 1:85-99.

Jezl, David R., Christian E. Molidor, and Tracy L. Wright. 1996. "Physical, Sexual, and Psychological Abuse in High School Dating Relationships: Prevalence Rates and Self-Esteem Issues." *Child and Adolescent Social Work Journal* 13:69-87.

Johnson, Michael P. 1995. "Patriarchal Terrorism and Common Couple Violence: Two Forms of Violence against Women." *Journal of Marriage and the Family* 57:283-294.

Johnson, Michael P. 2008. *A Typology of Domestic Violence: Intimate Terrorism, Violent Resistance, and Situational Couple Violence.* Boston, MA: Northeastern University Press.

Johnson, Michael P. 2010. "Langhinrichsen-Rolling's Confirmation of the Feminist Analysis of Intimate Partner Violence: Comment on "Controversies Involving Gender and Intimate Partner Violence in the United States." *Sex Roles* 62:212-219.

Johnson, Michael P. and Kathleen Ferraro. 2000. "Research on Domestic Violence in the 1990s: Making Distinctions." *Journal of Marriage and the Family* 62:948-963.

Johnston, Lloyd D., Patrick M. O'Malley, Jerald G. Bachman, and John E. Schulenberg. 2009. *Monitoring the Future National Survey Results on Drug Use, 1975-2008. Volume I: Secondary School Students.* NIH Publication No. 09-7402. Bethesda, MD: National Institute on Drug Abuse.

Kaighobadi, Farnaz, Todd K. Shackelford, and Aaron T. Goetz. 2009. "From Mate Retention to Murder: Evolutionary Psychological Perspectives on Men's Partner-Directed Violence." *Review of General Psychology* 13:327-334.

Kaufman Kantor, Glenda and Murray Straus. 1987. "The 'Drunken Bum' Theory of Wife Beating." *Social Problems* 34:213-230.

Kimmel, Michael S. 2002. "'Gender Symmetry' in Domestic Violence: A Substantive and Methodological Research Review." *Violence against Women* 8(11):1332-1363.

Klaus, Patsy A. 1994. *Costs of Crime to Victims.* Crime Data Brief. Washington, DC: U.S. Department of Justice, Office of Justice Programs, Bureau of Justice Statistics.

Kreager, Derek A. 2004. "Strangers in the Halls: Isolation and Delinquency in School Networks." *Social Forces* 83(1):351-390.

Larson, Reed and Douglas Kleiber. 1993. "Daily Experience of Adolescents." Pp. 125-145 in *Handbook of Clinical Research and Practice with Adolescents, Wiley Series on Personality Processes*, edited by Patrick H. Tolan and Bertram J. Cohler. New York, NY: John Wiley & Sons.

Lauritsen, Janet L. and Kenna F. Davis Quinet. 1995. "Repeat Victimization among Adolescents and Young Adults." *Journal of Quantitative Criminology* 11(2):143-166.

Lauritsen, Janet L., Robert J. Sampson, and John H. Laub. 1991. "The Link between Offending and Victimization among Adolescents." *Criminology* 29(2):265-292.

Levesque, Roger J. R. 1993. "The Romantic Experience of Adolescents in Satisfying Love Relationships." *Journal of Youth and Adolescence* 22:219-251.

Levinger, George. 1966. "Sources of Marital Dissatisfaction among Applicants for Divorce." *American Journal of Orthopsychiatry* 36:803-806.

Liao, Tim F. 1994. *Interpreting Probability Models: Logit, Probit, and Other Generalized Linear Models.* Thousand Oaks, CA: Sage.

Lurigio, Arthur J. 1987. "Are All Victims Alike? The Adverse, Generalized, and Differential Impact of Crime." *Crime and Delinquency* 33:452-467.

Macmillan, Ross and John Hagan. 2004. "Violence in the Transition to Adulthood: Adolescent Victimization, Education, and Socioeconomic Attainment in Later Life." *Journal of Research on Adolescence* 14(2):127-158.

Macmillan, Ross and Rosemary Gartner. 1999. "When She Brings Home the Bacon: Labor-Force Participation and the Risk of Spousal Violence against Women." *Journal of Marriage and the Family* 61:947–958.

Macmillan, Ross. 2000. "Adolescent Victimization and Income Deficits in Adulthood: Rethinking the Costs of Criminal Violence from a Life-Course Perspective." *Criminology* 38(2):553-588.

Macmillan, Ross. 2001. "Violence and the Life Course: The Consequences of Victimization for Personal and Social Development." *Annual Review of Sociology* 27:1-22.

Malik, Shaista, Susan B. Sorenson, and Carol S. Aneshensel. 1997. "Community and Dating Violence among Adolescents: Perpetration and Victimization." *Journal of Adolescent Health* 21(5):291-302.

Matsueda, Ross L. and Karen Heimer. 1987. "Race, Family Structure, and Delinquency: A Test of Differential Association and Social Control Theories." *American Sociological Review* 52: 826-840.

Mazerolle, Paul. 1998. "Gender, General Strain, and Delinquency: Empirical Examination." *Justice Quarterly 15*(1): 65-91.

McBurnett, Keith, Adrian Raine, Magda Stouthamer- Loeber, Rolf Loeber, Adarsh M. Kumar, and Benjamin B. Lahey. 2005. "Mood and Hormone Responses to Psychological Challenge in Adolescent Males with Conduct Problems." *Biological Psychiatry* 57:1109–1116.

McCarthy, Bill and Teresa Casey. 2008. "Love, Sex, and Crime: Adolescent Romantic Relationship and Offending." *American Sociological Review* 73:944-969.

McNeely, R. L. and CoraMae R. Mann. 1990. "Domestic Violence is a Human Issue." *Journal of Interpersonal Violence* 5:129-132.

Meier, Robert F. and Terance D. Miethe. 1993. "Understanding Theories of Criminal Victimization." *Crime and Justice* 17:459-499.

Meisel, Joan, Daniel Chandler, and Beth Menees Rienzi. 2003. "Domestic Violence Prevalence and Effects on Employment in Two California TANF Populations." *Violence against Women* 9(10):1191-1212.

Menard, Scott and David Huizinga. 2001. "Repeat Victimization in a High-Risk Neighborhood Sample of Adolescents." *Youth & Society* 32(4):447-472.

Menard, Scott. 2002. *Short- and Long-Term Consequences of Adolescent Victimization.* Bulletin. Washington, D.C.: U.S. Department of Justice, Office of Justice Programs, Office of Juvenile Justice and Delinquency Prevention Bulletin.

Merton, Robert. 1938. "Social Structure and Anomie." *American Sociological Review* 3:672-682.

Miethe, Terance D. and Robert F. Meier. 1994. *Crime and Its Social Context.* Albany, NY: SUNY Press.

Miethe, Terance D., Mark C. Stafford, and J. Scott Long. 1987. "Social Differentiation in Criminal Victimization: A Test of the Routine

Activities/Lifestyle Theory." *American Sociological Review* 52:184-194.

Miller, Jody. 1998. "Up it Up: Gender and the Accomplishment of Street Robbery." *Criminology* 36(1):37-66.

Miller, Jody. 2001. *One of the Guys: Girls, Gangs, and Gender.* New York, NY: Oxford University Press.

Miller, Ted R., Mark A. Cohen, and Brian Wiersema. 1996. *Victim Costs and Consequences: A New Look.* Washington, DC: U.S. Department of Justice, Office of Justice Programs, National Institute of Justice.

Mills, Linda G. 2003. *Insult to Injury: Rethinking Our Responses to Intimate Abuse.* Princeton, NJ: Princeton University Press.

Moffitt, Terrie E., Avshalom Caspi, Jay Belsky, and Phil A. Silva. 1992. "Childhood Experience and the Onset of Menarche: A Test of a Sociobiological Model." *Child Development* 63:47–58.

Moffitt, Terrie E., Robert F. Krueger, Avshalom Caspi, and Jeff Fagan. 2006. "Partner Abuse and General Crime: How are they the Same? How are they Different?" *Criminology* 38(1):199-232.

Molidor, Christian and Richard M. Tolman. 1998. "Gender and Contextual Factors in Adolescent Dating Violence." *Violence against Women* 4:180-194.

Montemayor, Raymond. 1982. "The Relationship between Parent-Adolescent Conflict and the Amount of Time Adolescents Spend Alone and With Parents and Peers." *Child Development* 53:1512-1519.

Morse, Barbara J. 1995. "Beyond the Conflict Tactics Scale: Assessing Gender Differences in Partner Violence." *Violence and Victims* 10:251-272.

Mulford, Carrie and Peggy C. Giordano. 2008. "Teen Dating Violence: A Closer Look at Adolescent Romantic Relationships." *National Institute of Justice Journal* 261:34-40.

National Center for Injury Prevention and Control. 2006. "Dating Abuse Fact Sheet." Centers for Disease Control, Retrieved November, 1st 2008. (http://www.cdc.gov/ncipc/dvp/datingviolence.htm)

Norris, Fran H., and Krzysztof Kaniasty. 1991. "The psychological experience of crime: A test of the mediating role of beliefs in explaining the distress of victims." *Journal of Social and Clinical Psychology* 10:239-261.

Norris, Fran H., Krzysztof Kaniasty, and Martie P. Thompson. 1997. "The Psychological Consequences of Crime: Findings from a Longitudinal Population-Based Study." Pp. 146-166 in *Victims of Crime, Second Edition,* edited by Robert C. Davis, Arthur J. Lurigio, and Wesley G. Skogan. Thousand Oaks, CA: Sage Publications.

Nunnally, Jum C. 1978. *Psychometric Theory: Second Edition.* New York, NY: McGraw-Hill.

Nye, F. Ivan and James F. Short, Jr. 1957. "Scaling Delinquent Behavior." *American Sociological Review* 22:326-331.

O'Brien, John E. 1971. "Violence in Divorce-Prone Families." *Journal of Marriage and the Family* 33:692-698.

O'Keefe, Maura. 1997. "Predictors of Dating Violence among High School Students." *Journal of Interpersonal Violence* 12(4):546-568.

O'Leary, K. Daniel, Amy M. Smith Slep, and Susan G. O'Leary. 2007. "Multivariate Models of Men's and Women's Partner Aggression." *Journal of Consulting and Clinical Psychology* 75(5):752-764.

O'Leary, K. Daniel, Amy M. Smith Slep, Sarah Avery-Leaf, and Michele Cascardi. 2008. "Gender Differences in Dating Aggression among Multiethnic High School Students." *Journal of Adolescent Health* 42:473-479.

Ogle, Robbin S., Daniel Maier-Katkin, and Thomas J. Bernard. 1995. "A Theory of Homicidal Behavior among Women." *Criminology* 33(2):173-193.

Olshen, Elyse, Katharine H. McVeigh, Robin A. Wunsch-Hitzig and Vaughn I. Rickert. 2007. "Dating Violence, Sexual Assault, and Suicide Attempts Among Urban Teenagers." *Archives of Pediatrics and Adolescent Medicine* 161(6):539-545.

Olson, Elizabeth. "A Rise in Efforts to Spot Abuse in Youth Dating." *The New York Times*, January 3, 2009. Retrieved March 10, 2009. (http://www.nytimes.com/2009/01/04/us/04abuse.html)

Osborn, Denise R. and Andromachi Tseloni. 1998. "The Distribution of Household Property Crimes." *Journal of Quantitative Criminology* 14(3):307-330.

Osgood, D. Wayne, Janet K. Wilson, Patrick M. O'Malley, Jerald G. Bachman, and Lloyd D. Johnston. 1996. "Routine Activities and

Individual Deviant Behavior." *American Sociological Review* 61:635-655.

Osgood, D.Wayne, Barbara J. McMorris, and Maria T. Potenza. 2002. "Analyzing Multiple-Item Measures of Crime and Deviance: Item Response Theory Scaling." *Journal of Quantitative Criminology* 18:267-296.

Paternoster, Raymond, Robert Brame, Paul Mazerolle, and Alex Piquero. 1998. "Using the Correct Statistical Test for the Equality of Regression Coefficients." *Criminology* 36(4): 859-866.

Pence, Ellen and Michael Paymar. 1993. *Education Groups for Men Who Batter: The Duluth Model.* New York, NY: Springer.

Perkins, Craig, Patsy Klaus, Lisa Bastian, and Robyn Cohen. 1996. *Criminal Victimization in the United States, 1993.* Special Report. Washington, D.C.: U.S. Department of Justice, Office of Justice Programs, Bureau of Justice Statistics.

Peters, Jay, Todd K. Shackelford, and David M. Buss. 2002. "Understanding Domestic Violence against Women: Using Evolutionary Psychology to Extend the Feminist Functional Analysis." *Violence and Victims* 17:255-264.

Piquero, Nicole Leeper and Miriam D. Sealock. 2004. "Gender and General Strain Theory: A Preliminary Test of Broidy and Agnew's Gender/GST Hypotheses." *Justice Quarterly* 21:125-158.

Rand, Michael R. 1997. *Violence-Related Injuries Treated in Hospital Emergency Departments.* Special Report. Washington, D.C.: U.S. Department of Justice, Office of Justice Programs, Bureau of Justice Statistics.

Rennison, Callie M. and Sarah Welchans. 2000. *Intimate Partner Violence.* Special Report. Washington, D.C.: U.S. Department of Justice, Office of Justice Programs, Bureau of Justice Statistics.

Rennison, Callie M. 2003. *Intimate Partner Violence, 1993-2001.* Crime Data Brief. Washington, D.C.: U.S. Department of Justice, Office of Justice Programs, Bureau of Justice Statistics.

Resick, Patricia A. and Pallavi Nishith. 1997. "Sexual Assault." Pp. 27-52 in *Victims of Crime, Second Edition*, edited by Robert C. Davis, Arthur J. Lurigio, and Wesley G. Skogan. Thousand Oaks, CA: Sage Publications.

Reuterman, Nicholas A. and William D. Burcky. 1989. "Dating Violence in High School: A Profile of the Victims." *Psychology: A Journal of Human Behavior* 26(4):1-9.

Roberts, Timothy A., Jonathan D. Klein, and Susan Fisher. 2003. "Longitudinal Effect of Intimate Partner Abuse on High-Risk Behavior among Adolescents." *Archives of Pediatrics and Adolescent Medicine* 157(4):857-881.

Roscoe, Bruce and John E. Callahan. 1985. "Adolescents' Self-Report of Violence in Families and Dating Relations." *Adolescence* 20:545-554.

Rosenthal, Robert, Ralph L. Rosnow, and Donald B. Rubin. 2000. *Contrasts and Effect Sizes in Behavioral Research: A Correlational Approach.* Cambridge: Cambridge University Press.

Sampson, Robert J. and Janet L. Lauritsen. 1990. "Deviant Lifestyles, Proximity to Crime, and the Offender-Victim Link in Personal Violence." *Journal of Research in Crime and Delinquency* 27(2):110-139.

Sampson, Robert J. and Janet L. Lauritsen. 1994. "Violent Victimization and Offending: Individual-, Situational-, and Community-level Risk Factors." Pp. 1-114 in *Understanding and Preventing Violence, Volume 3: Social Influences*, edited by Albert J. Reiss and Jeffrey A. Roth. Washington, D.C.: National Research Council, National Academy Press.

Schafer, John, Raul Caetano, and Catherine L. Clark. 1998. "Rates of Intimate Partner Violence in the United States." *American Journal of Public Health* 88(11):1702-1704.

Schreck, Christopher J. and Bonnie S. Fisher. 2004. "Specifying the Influence of Family and Peers on Violent Victimization." *Journal of Interpersonal Violence* 19(9):1021-1041.

Schreck, Christopher J., Eric A. Stewart, and Bonnie S. Fisher. 2006. "Self-Control, Victimization, and their Influence on Risky Lifestyles: A Longitudinal Analysis using Panel Data." *Journal of Quantitative Criminology* 22(4):319-340.

Schreck, Christopher J., Eric A. Stewart, and D. Wayne Osgood. 2008. "A Reappraisal of the Overlap of Violent Offenders and Victims." *Criminology* 46(4):871-906.

Schreck, Christopher J., J. Mitchell Miller, and Chris L. Gibson. 2003. "Trouble in the School Yard: A Study of the Risk Factors of Victimization at School." *Crime & Delinquency* 49(3):460-484.

Shaffer, Jennifer N. and R. Barry Ruback. 2002. *Violent Victimization as a Risk Factor for Violent Offending Among Juveniles.* Bulletin. Washington, D.C.: U.S. Department of Justice, Office of Justice Programs, Office of Juvenile Justice and Delinquency Prevention.

Silverman, Jay G., Anita Raj, Lorelei A. Mucci, and Jeanne E. Hathaway. 2001. "Dating Violence against Adolescent Girls and Associated Substance Use, Unhealthy Weight Control, Sexual Risk Behavior, Pregnancy, and Suicidality." *Journal of the American Medical Association* 286(5):572-579.

Simons, Ronald L., Christine Johnson, Jay Beaman, and Rand D. Conger. 1993. "Explaining Women's Double Jeopardy: Factors that Mediate the Association between Harsh Treatment as a Child and Violence by a Husband." *Journal of Marriage and Family* 55(3):713-723.

Sinha, Rajita. 2001. "How Does Stress Increase Risk of Drug Abuse and Relapse?" *Psychopharmacology* 158:343–359.

Skinner, B. F. 1953. *Science and Human Behavior.* New York: Macmillan.

Stark, Evan. 2007. *Coercive Control: The Entrapment of Women in Personal Life.* Oxford: Oxford University Press.

Steffensmeier, Darrell and Emilie Allan. 1996. "Gender and Crime: Toward a Gendered Theory of Female Offending." *Annual Review of Sociology* 22:459-487.

Steinmetz, Suzanne K. 1987. "Family Violence: Past, Present, and Future." Pp. 725-765 in *Handbook of Marriage and the Family*, edited by Marvin B. Sussman and Suzanne K. Steinmetz. New York, NY: Plenum Press.

Steinmetz, Suzanne K. and Joseph S. Lucca. 1988. "Husband Battering." Pp. 61-87 in *Handbook of Family Violence*, edited by Vincent B. Van Hasselt, Randall L. Morrison, Alan S. Bellack, and Michel Hersen. New York, NY: Plenum Press.

Stets, Jan E. and Murray A. Straus. 1990. "Gender Differences in Reporting Marital Violence and its Medical and Psychological Consequences." Pp. 151-166 in *Physical Violence in American Families: Risk Factors and Adaptations to Violence in 8,145 Families*, edited by Murray A. Straus and Richard J. Gelles. New Brunswick, NJ: Transaction Publishers.

Stiffman, Arlene R. 1989. "Physical and Sexual Abuse in Runaway Youths." *Child Abuse and Neglect* 13:417–426.

Straus Murray A. and Richard J. Gelles. 1986. "Societal Change and Family Violence from 1975 to 1985 as Revealed by Two National Surveys." *Journal of Marriage and the Family* 48:445-479.

Straus Murray A. and Richard J. Gelles. 1990. "How Violent are American Families? Estimates from the National Family Violence Resurvey and Other Studies." Pp. 95-112 in *Physical Violence in American Families: Risk Factors and Adaptations to Violence in 8,145 Families,* edited by Murray A. Straus and Richard J. Gelles. New Brunswick, NJ: Transaction Publishers.

Straus, Murray A. 1977. "Wife-Beating: How Common, and Why?" *Victimology* 2:443-458.

Straus, Murray A. 1980. "The Marriage License as a Hitting License: Evidence from Popular Culture, Law, and Social Science." Pp. 39-50 in *The Social Causes of Husband-Wife Violence*, edited by Murray A. Straus and Gerald T. Hotaling. Minneapolis, MN: University of Minnesota Press.

Straus, Murray A. 1990. "Measuring Intrafamily Conflict and Violence: The Conflict Tactics (CT) Scales." Pp. 29-47 in *Physical Violence in American Families: Risk Factors and Adaptations to Violence in 8,145 Families,* edited by Murray A. Straus and Richard J. Gelles. New Brunswick, NJ: Transaction Publishers.

Straus, Murray A. 1997. "Physical Assaults by Women Partners: A Major Social Problem." Pp. 204-221 in *Women, Men, and Gender: Ongoing Debates*, edited by Mary Roth Walsh. New Haven, CT: Yale University Press.

Straus, Murray A. 1999. "The Controversy Over Domestic Violence by Women: A Methodological, Theoretical, and Sociology of Science Analysis." Pp. 17-44 in *Violence in Intimate Relationships*, edited by Ximena B. Arriaga and Stuart Oskamp. Thousand Oaks, CA: Sage.

Sutherland, Edwin H. and Donald R. Cressey. 1955. *Principles of Criminology, Fifth Edition.* Philadelphia, PA: J.B. Lippincott.

Sutherland, Edwin H., Donald R. Cressey, and David F. Luckenbill. 1934 (1992). *Principles of Criminology.* New York, NY: General Hall.

Sweet, James, Larry Bumpass, and Vaughn Call. 1988. "The Design and Content of the National Survey of Families and Households,

NSFH Working Paper 1." Madison: University of Wisconsin, Center for Demography and Ecology.

Sweeting, Helen, Robert Young, Patrick West, and Geoff Der. 2006. "Peer Victimization and Depression in Early-Mid Adolescence: A Longitudinal Study." *British Journal of Educational Psychology* 76(3):577-594.

Tjaden, Patricia and Nancy Thoennes. 1998. *Prevalence, Incidence, and Consequences of Violence against Women: Findings from the National Violence Against Women Survey.* Research Report (No. NCJ 172837). Washington, D.C.: U.S. Department of Justice, Office of Justice Programs, National Institute of Justice.

Tjaden, Patricia and Nancy Thoennes. 2000. *Extent, Nature, and Consequences of Intimate Partner Violence: Findings from the National Violence against Women Survey.* Research Report. Washington, D.C.: U.S. Department of Justice, Office of Justice Programs, National Institute of Justice.

United States Federal Bureau of Investigation. 2005. *Violence among Family Members and Intimate Partners.* Retrieved March 10, 2009. (http://www.fbi.gov/ucr/cius_03/pdf/03sec5.pdf)

Warr, Mark and Mark Stafford. 1991. "The Influence of Delinquent Peers: What They Think or What They Do?" *Criminology* 29:851-865.

Warr, Mark. 1993. "Age, Peers, and Delinquency." *Criminology* 31:17-40.

Warr, Mark. 1998. "Life-Course Transitions and Desistance from Crime." *Criminology* 36:183-216.

Warr, Mark. 2002. *Companions in Crime: The Social Aspects of Criminal Conduct.* Cambridge: Cambridge University Press.

Wekerle, Christine and David A. Wolfe. 1999. "Dating Violence in Mid-Adolescence: Theory, Significance, and Emerging Prevention Initiatives." *Child Psychology Review* 19(4):435-456.

Widom, Cathy Spatz. 1989. "The Cycle of Violence." *Science* 244:160-166.

Wittebrood, Karin and Paul Nieuwbeerta. 2000. "Criminal Victimization During One's Life Course: The Effects of Previous Victimization and Patterns of Routine Activities." *Journal of Research in Crime and Delinquency* 37:91-122.

Zahn, Margaret A., Robert Agnew, Diana Fishbein, Shari Miller, Donna-Marie Winn, Gayle Dakoff, Candace Kruttschnitt, Peggy Giordano, Denise C. Gottfredson, Allison A. Payne, Barry C. Feld, and Meda Chesney-Lind. 2010. *Causes and Correlates of Girls' Delinquency.* Girls Study Group: Understanding and Responding to Girls Delinquency. Washington, D.C.:U.S. Department of Justice, Office of Justice Programs Office of Juvenile Justice and Delinquency Prevention.

Index

violent resistance (VR), 10-
    12, 21, 147, 179
situational couple violence
    (SCV). 10-12, 21, 147,
    179, 189, 191
Kimmel, Michael S., 5-9
Lauritsen, Janet L., 18, 26, 35, 36,
    51, 55, 180, 190
Logistic Regression, 64, 77-78,
    97-98, 101, 103, 106,
    129, 131, 136, 142, 149
Mazerolle, Paul, 27, 29, 44
Meier, Robert F., 33-34, 36-37
Merton, Robert, 40-41
Miethe, Terance D., 33-34, 36-37
Miller, Jody, 27-29, 47, 144, 185
Missing Data, 69, 73-76, 151, 179
    missing at random (MAR),
        74-75
    missing completely at
        random (MCAR), 74-75
    non-ignorable (NI), 74-75
Mulford, Carrie, 1-2, 12, 14-16,
    20, 47
Multinomial regression, 78, 148,
    162-163
Multiple imputation, 62, 69, 73-
    77, 149
National Crime Victimization
    Survey (NCVS), 4, 9
National Family Violence Survey
    (NFVS), 6-8
National Incident Based Reporting
    System (NIBRS), 4
National Longitudinal Study of
    Adolescent Health (Add
    Health), 3, 15, 17, 21,
    32, 49, 55-80, 95, 109,

111, 147-149, 159, 179-
    181, 184-185, 190-192
National Violence against Women
    Survey (NVAW), 4-5, 9
Negative binomial regression 68,
    77-78, 121-123, 125,
    128, 133-135, 138-139,
    141, 167
Nieuwbeerta, Paul, 17, 51, 180,
    190
Olshen, Elyse, 15-17, 29, 44
Opportunity theories, 33-41, 48-
    49, 52, 99, 109, 180-
    181, 189
    lifestyle exposure theory, 33-
        38, 50, 109-110, 180,
        189
    routine activities theory, 33-
        35, 38-39, 48
Patriarchy, 12-14, 25, 26
Paymar, Michael, 11
Pence, Ellen, 11
Poisson modeling, 67, 77, 148,
    167, 169, 170, 172
Population heterogeneity, 51, 190
Quinet, Kenna F. Davis, 36, 51,
    190
Ruback, R. Barry, 18, 24, 31, 40,
    56, 82, 181
Sampson, Robert J., 18, 36, 180
Schreck, Christopher J., 17-18, 23,
    36, 180
Shaffer, Jennifer N., 18, 24, 31,
    40, 56, 82, 181
Social Learning Theories, 13, 33,
    45-49, 109
    Differential Association
        Theory, 33, 45-50